GW00648746

Embodied Education

Creating Safe Space for Learning, Facilitating and Sharing

Kay Louise Aldred and Dan Aldred

Cover Art by Andrew Swiatkowski

ISBN: 9788293725466

Disclaimer and Caution

Please note that none of the information presented in this book is meant to replace the advice of a medical, health, legal and/or any other professional or service. How you choose to act on the words and content is of your own determination and free will.

Finally, this manual contains references and content relating to trauma. This may trigger and activate you and your nervous system. Please take good care of yourself and others as you work through this manual. Do the wellbeing, nervous system regulatory, and somatic exercises outlined in the book. If anything comes up personally for you or others which is beyond your capacity to deal with, lean into your support networks and services, and remember your GP is a good place to start should you need additional help. You can stop reading at any time. Taking breaks and pausing frequently during reading is recommended, as it helps to process and integrate the material.

Praise for Embodied Education

"This is the most inspiring and exciting book I have ever read on education and facilitation.

The Aldred's are proposing a much-needed revolution in education; one that is body first, relational and heart-led. Their focus on embodiment, wellbeing, co-regulation and creativity is exactly what is needed for our complex world today.

The synergy of neurotypical and neurodivergent perspectives provides a radical pedagogy and facilitation approach suitable for all kinds of learners.

Everyone will benefit from their embodied approach, especially the invaluable information on trauma, stress and regulating the nervous system.

The extensive expertise and experience of Kay and Dan, as educators, shines through, as does their passion, wisdom and massive spirit of service.

This is a groundbreaking book, with a powerful vision and curriculum, in direct contrast to the outdated and energy draining curriculum most school children have to endure on a daily basis. I will personally send a copy to the UK Secretary of State for Education to influence education policy in my own country.

I urge every teacher, parent and facilitator to read this book to enable the much-needed change, both within and outside the formal education system.

It will also inspire those who are home schooling and facilitating within a wide range of contexts. This is the book I have been waiting for to refresh and further inform my own teaching and coaching. I first completed my teacher training in 1980 and I have read and experimented extensively within education and pedagogy ever since.

I place this book on a par with the best educational books ever written. Especially ones that challenge the status quo and offer a radical, workable, wise and significant alternative. An extraordinary contribution to the world of learning."

-Dr Lynne Sedgmore CBE, Former secondary school teacher, college lecturer and college Principal. Previous CEO of the Centre of Excellence in Leadership. Author and tutor of *Goddess Luminary Leadership Wheel*, and *Presence Activism* (to be published in 2024).

"This courageous book is a primer for these times. I want every educator, and every student, to have access to these resources. Having just created MA and PhD curricula, I have taken the concepts of somatic, embodied education expressed in this book to heart.

This book is a fundamental orientation towards any pedagogy or wisdom transmission. This is a time when we need mentors to be strong, real and present and to win the respect of their students who crave guidance and who cannot be deceived. We need the real thing, and this book has it.

The practical exercises in Embodied Education are a potent somatic curriculum for transforming all learning experience into relevance."

-Stephanie Mines, PhD, Author of *The Secret of Resilience*. Developer of Regenerative Health for A Climate Changing World, Fellow of the Planetary Health Lab of the University of Edinburgh

"Kay's work on understanding regulation has been hugely influential in my work, and I'm excited to see Kay and Dan translate this learning for education settings.

Embodied Education provides an accessible overview to important theory, and practical exercises to support this learning to be applied.

Understanding the nervous system and supporting regulation is the 'missing piece' for many neurodivergent people, whose dysregulation is misunderstood and met with behavioural interventions.

I'm delighted to be able to recommend this book to educators, as it provides insight and alternative approaches that will support connection, safety, and improved outcomes that can be transformative for both practitioners and the young people they support."

-Jill Corbyn, Founder and Director of Neurodiverse Connection and the lead author on the co-produced 'It's Not Rocket Science' report into inpatient sensory environments and LGA paper 'Supporting autistic flourishing at home and beyond: considering and meeting the sensory needs of autistic people in housing'.

"Reading from the lens of peace and conflict resolution, *Embodied Education* is such a deep and considered manual that would be invaluable for trainers working in either post conflict communities, or with refugee communities who have experienced the unimaginable. By placing the body and trauma informed methodologies at the heart of the learning practice - this manual offers many keys to unlock learning for people who are keen to rebuild and learn but need safe space and an embodied practice to do so. The artwork is incredible too!"
-Dr Sarah Alldred, PhD in Peace Studies and Conflict Resolution (2003). Currently the Head of International Partnership, The Co-operative College, Manchester.

Contents

Disclaimer and Caution 2

Praise for Embodied Education 3

INTRODUCTION: Embodied Education **7**

Welcome 12

Embodied Education – The Model 14

How to use this Manual 15

Before you Start 17

Definitions 24

Dedication 27

THE FOUNDATIONAL BASICS **30**

Essential Understanding of the Nervous System, Stress and Trauma 31

What is Trauma? 36

Importance of limbic resonance and coregulation 38

Practicing the Pause of Presence – 3-step process 39

What it Means to be Trauma-informed 41

Basic Wellness – Essential Bodily Needs 47

Embodied Mindfulness 51

Self-Compassion 52

Body Intelligence 55

Gut Instinct and The Ick 56

Impulse 57

Intuition 58

Attachment Theory 59

Safety 61

Safe Relating 63

Boundaries 65

Power 67

Navigating the Change – What it Looks Like in Practice 71

THE SPACE **72**

Systems, Policies and Procedures 73

The Building Itself 77

Interpersonal Dynamics 80

External Inspection 83

Referral Pathways 85

Navigating the Change – What it Looks Like in Practice 87

THE SPACE HOLDER 88

Red Flags 92

Responsibility 94

Supervision 97

How to Relate 99

THE CONTENT 102

Body ABCs and Mind 103

Exercise 1: The SOS 105

Exercise 2: Building Capacity 106

Exercise 3: The Maintenance – ongoing regular practice 107

Supporting the Mind to Support the Nervous System – Laying the Foundations 110

Self-Leadership 114

Creativity 116

Language 118

Undo the Patriarchy 120

Navigating the Change – What it Looks Like in Practice 123

THE PEDAGOGY **124**

Creative Curiosity 125

Critical Thinking 127

Storytelling 129

Metacognition 131

Intuition 133

Instinct 135

Navigating the Change – What it Looks Like in Practice 136

CONCLUSION **137**

About the Artists 139

About the Authors 140

Further Exploration: Embodied Education 141

Thanks to the Survey Respondents 143

Other Thanks 144

Introduction: Embodied Education

What is our vision?

Embodied Education is our vision for an educational paradigm based on wellbeing, co-regulation and creativity. We advocate for body-first, relational and embodied approaches in organisations and communities.

We write this book as a neurotypical and neurodivergent, male and female partnership, offering a diverse yet complimentary compendium of ideas and experience. We endeavour to fuse masculine and feminine energetics and models of leadership through a union of mind, body and heart led direction.

Our aims are to support a shift in culture to an embodied, holistic model of learning, facilitating and sharing, by raising awareness, supporting curiosity and suggesting alternatives and solutions.

We champion the creation of spaces which are trauma-informed and neurodivergent, sensory and nervous system friendly. We support, celebrate and encourage individuality, divergence and innovation, alongside exploration, discovery and imagination. We consider intuition (in addition to metacognition and critical thinking) to be a go-to point of reference and above all else, we believe gut instinct has the final say.

Why this vision?

This combination of traits is essential to sustain a thriving learning environment and organisation – whether that be a school, hospital, social care setting, wellness or spiritual community. Communication is easeful, everybody has their needs met, and learning and creativity prosper. Our person-centred mentorship approach is focused on growth, wellness and innovation for all learners and staff alike. Nurturing open mindsets, we foster a culture of celebration of authentic self-expression and achievement. Each person is well and whole, their individual abilities, strengths and gifts are praised and grown, whilst areas for development are addressed.

Fundamentally we believe humans are all born spirited and unique, each with their own distinctive and individual ways of learning. Youngsters and adults, when connected to their inner child – their inborn curiosity, awe and wonder – naturally problem solve, know when to ask for help and actively seek to discover the answers to the question *why?* As children develop, they willingly participate in learning literacy and numeracy schemas and see the value of rudimentary educational building blocks, absorbing the modelling they receive, to scaffold their experimentation and deepen their exploration. Innately, we are all destined to be curious and want to learn and grow. Our experience has taught us that there is no greater privilege than undertaking the role of educator, space holder and facilitator, supporting and nurturing this bloom.

Our vision is for body-first organisations and a learning paradigm based on wellbeing, embodiment, collaboration, creativity, and innovation – privilege is translated into service for the community and environment, and where learners embed into their minds, bodies and hearts the unshakeable foundations of self-belief – from knowing the truth of who they are and the value of their unique offering to this ever-changing world. Exceptional learning and growth organically flow from body comfort and regulated nervous system. These conditions activate curiosity and discovery, connection and resilience. Impactful learning will only take place if the nervous system has capacity and regulation.

Children and adults alike build resilience and capacity in their nervous systems, or otherwise, in relationship with adults facilitating the space. If adults who are leading, teaching, or space holding are stressed, children and adults participating in the space are stressed – and learning and growth are compromised.

Outstanding learning and care start with well, embodied and regulated children and adults – which starts with well, embodied and regulated staff – which starts with well, embodied and regulated leaders. *This is what we are committed to being.* We embody, lead, and behave by example. In a nervous system friendly, trauma-informed, embodied organisation, learning, facilitation and space holding is progressive, cutting-edge and the new paradigm being birthed through us – and is especially needed in the wake of the Covid 19 pandemic.

From our wide range of community, regional, national and international work and combined life experiences, we have come to understand that regardless of age, background or demographic, humans have four basic needs to thrive.

They are – to be *seen, heard, valued*, and *safe*.

Why write this?

As mature and long-serving teachers and educators, we have witnessed a gradual year-on-year deterioration of young people's mental health, self-belief and confidence – and a suffocation of their inquisitiveness, ability to learn independently and desire to thrive. By the time many young people reach secondary school they are in the process of 'shut down.' Patterns of dissociation, disaffectedness and apathy are often well-established and any flame of longing and desire to learn has been extinguished. Children who do not match the 'one size fits all' approach are often regarded as *at fault* or *lacking*.

We would argue, however, that it is the narrow scope and uniformity of the system, (accessible to a limited number of students only), which has actually failed them. The current system is not working, and neither is it fit for purpose or preference. In 2020 the independent journalism UK-focused charity, Each Other, reported that 'Government statistics show that permanent exclusions have increased by 71% in the UK in the last seven years.'[1] Young people and their families are also voting with their feet against is. An article in *The Guardian* newspaper reported

---

[1] https://eachother.org.uk/11-facts-you-should-know-about-school-exclusions/

in November 2021 that local councils in England were reporting a '34% rise in elective home education.' [2]

The purpose of this manual is to provide an examination of the issues related to 'disembodied' learning and suggest alternatives and solutions. Our aim is to facilitate a shift in culture and approach towards an embodied, holistic model by raising awareness of the problems and supporting curiosity. Additionally, we want to create safe and trauma-informed spaces for embodied learning and facilitation, where individuality, divergence, and innovation are valued, celebrated, and encouraged. We believe that exploration, discovery, and creativity should be the foundational values in these spaces. We also acknowledge that making mistakes is a natural part of the learning process, and intuition is considered an essential point of reference. Finally, we believe that gut instinct should have the final say in decision-making.

We write this manual to bring the body back to education and learning spaces which have not been reformed for a considerable length of time.

Who are we?

We write this book as two people experienced in teaching, leadership, school governance, facilitation, space holding, pastoral care, counselling, coaching, therapeutic support, creative enterprise, content and resource production, writing, volunteering, mentoring and parenting of neurodivergent children. We also write as a neurotypical husband and neurodivergent wife team, skilled in neurodiverse connection and inter-neurotype communication.

What we can boldly say from the outset is that spaces where learning, facilitation and sharing are taking place (whether that be mainstream or home-schooling environments, health or social care services, personal development forums, spiritual and wellness communities) – are, on the whole, disembodied.

Who are we writing for?

Our initial focus was educational establishments but as the manual evolved, we saw that the content was applicable across most of the areas and institutions in society. We are writing to support the navigation of change and the bridging of old to new paradigms.

So, we write for teachers and school leaders, home, unschooling or alternative educational provision teachers and facilitators, health and social care practitioners – and for anyone facilitating a space where sharing and learning takes place – including religion, charities and personal development, wellness and spiritual arenas, which have seen an explosion of teaching, courses and content being widely shared and sold.

Based on our personal and professional experience, we also recognise that all aspects of facilitator, health and social care practitioner and teacher wellbeing is in decline. There is an

---

[2] https://www.theguardian.com/education/2021/nov/24/councils-england-report-34-rise-elective-home-education-children

epidemic of compassion fatigue[3] and burn out[4] in health care settings. In education settings, many teachers continue to ignore the body signals of potential burnout for fear of losing their job or being seen as not being able to cope and being judged for needing support. This was clearly illustrated in the August 2022 edition of *Teaching Today NASUWT Members' Magazine* which published the following results from their Big Question Survey 2022 which was completed by nearly 15,000 union members:

- 81% feel their job has adversely affected their mental health in the last 12 months.
- 83% experience anxiousness.
- 79% experience loss of sleep.
- 69% experience irritability/mood swings.
- 68% experience low energy levels.
- 66% of members have considered leaving the teaching profession in the last year.

Our intention is that *Embodied Education* will support service sustainability and the wellbeing of everyone, including the practitioners, carers, and those facilitating, teaching or space holding.

Why these topics?

We recognise and are committed to the need for structures, learning and sharing spaces and organisations in society. Structures provide boundaries and a container for energy to be channelled and for humans to feel safe, be curious and creative, and flourish. Learning environments offer the building blocks and framework for exploration and discovery. However, based on our personal and professional experience (and the informal feedback we received), the fencing of these spaces needs to be redesigned and reformed.

We fundamentally believe in the premise of *first do no harm* and because we see harm being done in education, health, social care, wellness, personal development and spiritual contexts we felt compelled to write this. We also firmly advocate that the mind needs the body, and the body needs the mind for humans to grow and expand. In our opinion, any system that leaves either out – or marginalises one over the other – is creating division and dis-ease in a person. We argue that both the mind and the body are vehicles of knowledge, awareness, growth and learning.

Therefore, we write about the magic of creativity, in addition to the thriving, power and resilience which is born from the cultivation of an internal locus of control – natural by-products arising from any space where there is a unity of metacognition, intuition and instinct.

---

[3] https://www.theguardian.com/society/2020/jan/27/third-of-uk-doctors-report-burnout-and-compassion-fatigue
[4] https://www.nhsemployers.org/articles/beating-burnout-nhs

Who is this manual for?

This manual is for:

- Anyone who holds space, one-on-one or in a group setting.
- Anywhere space holding, facilitation, education or learning takes place.
- Anywhere information is exchanged.

This includes (but isn't limited to) the following venues and arenas: schools, universities, youth work, teaching, home-schooling, unschooling, health and social care services, wellness, women's circles, men's groups, self-development, night classes, befriending services, charities, social justice, parenting, holistic health and therapeutic settings, religion and spiritual spaces.

The information and approaches in this book can be used by an individual, a group or a whole organisation.

Can the Embodied Education model and approaches be implemented even if the organisation or service isn't supporting change?

Yes!

What to do in this scenario

Change begins with us – all of us, individually – building more capacity and regulation into our nervous system, creating more safety in our own bodies first. Grass roots change, a bottom-up approach, is totally aligned with the principles of Embodied Education. Individual change ripples out and creates a resonance of safety and embodiment which vibrates throughout the organisation. So just start. Read the manual. Do the practises. Be the change and see what happens.

By practicing the principles outlined in our book, you will experience personal benefits and improve your work and interactions with your students, clients, and those you hold space for. It's possible that those in leadership positions may ask questions about what you're doing differently. In that case, we encourage you to share your experiences with them. By embodying these principles, you'll become a positive example of change, and your embodiment will have a magnetic quality that draws others towards it. We know this from our own personal experience.

As far as resources go, we have included a *Further Exploration* page which lists suggested websites and reading. You may also follow us on social media or visit our websites to find out more about the work we do.

Welcome

"It is nothing short of a miracle that modern methods of instruction have not yet entirely strangled the holy curiosity of inquiry."

Albert Einstein [5]

Curiosity is the fuel for joy and for feeling fully alive. We agree with Einstein who also said, "The important thing is not to stop questioning – curiosity has its own reason for existing"[6] Curiosity is the elixir of pleasure and happiness as it offers newness and discovery, novelty and growth in every moment. It prevents stagnation (and we'd even suggest ill health), the suppression of creativity (our expression of power), and safeguards against depression and hopelessness.

To spark curiosity, to foster exploration and discovery, to share ideas and to nurture the creative and intellectual lifeforce of young men and women – these are the reasons we both followed our vocation and entered into the profession of teaching.

And so, when we finally paused – after nearly 50 years of combined experience in education, facilitation and space holding – and fully opened our eyes, we perceived that the current formal educational paradigm, which we had been perpetuating and colluding with – was annihilating the spirit of children and adults alike, eradicating their curiosity, stamping out their originality, shaming their quirkiness and extinguishing their creativity.

Understandably, on seeing this we felt angry and sorrowful. We spent many hours questioning and discussing the value of everything we spent our professional lives devoted to. *What had we done? What choices did we make and why?* Had these actions resonated with us or were we simply enmeshed in a rigid systematic structure that disregarded human intuition and blinded us to its input and messages? Why had we simply run on autopilot, fulfilling the expectations of the role without reflection or consideration? We felt moved to investigate and find out if we were the only ones asking questions... thinking and feeling that the education system was failing – and in fact causing harm.

We discovered that we were not alone. Our survey respondents described the current education system as 'competitive' (71.1%), 'goal-driven' (66%), 'controlled' (69.8%), 'demanding' (67.9%), 'critical' (64.2%) and driven by 'dominance' (64.2%). The YMCA charity website in 2016 featured an article on the 'negative educational experiences cause lasting damage to wellbeing' [7] which was based on the findings of their Eudaimonia research report.

Sir Ken Robinson, an educator, author and speaker, stated in his 2006 TED Talk, 'Do Schools Kill Creativity?' that schools and our education system have mined our minds in the same way that

---

[5] https://www.institute4learning.com/2020/01/15/14-great-quotes-from-einstein-on-education-with-sources/

[6] https://www.institute4learning.com/2020/01/15/14-great-quotes-from-einstein-on-education-with-sources/

[7] https://www.ymca.co.uk/health-and-wellbeing/feature/negative-educational-experiences-cause-lasting-damage-wellbeing

we strip-mine the earth for a particular commodity. And for the future, it won't serve us. We have to rethink the fundamental principles on which we're educating our children."[8] This TED Talk has been viewed over 74 million times, so clearly it resonates with many.

The question of who actually decides and directs what we 'should' learn is shady – and these decisions are frequently made by academics who are completely out of sync with students' interests. From our experience, there are government directives driven by an agenda of implanting into young people the narratives of patriarchy, capitalism, consumerism and extraction.

Many current educational spaces are predominantly fear-based, hierarchical, head-only and dissociative – places where unsafe relating occurs, as teachers often act out their own school trauma and patterning. We've noticed that the same issues that occur in traditional schooling environments can also arise in other spaces where people gather to learn and grow, such as personal development or spiritual arenas. This was something that Kay experienced first-hand after leaving mainstream education. Navigating these spaces can be even more challenging, especially if they are gender segregated.

Bullying continues in spiritual communities, spaces and practises. Patriarchal conditioning and school wounding is active in sharing circles. What was programmed in us at school – that we are never good enough, need to try harder, study more, achieve more – is being hijacked and monopolised by the wellness and personal growth industry, which tells us that we are broken and defective.

This manual will unpack all of these issues in more detail. As we said earlier, our goal is to support a shift in culture and approach to an embodied, holistic model by providing an examination of the issues related to embodied learning and suggest alternatives and solutions. Our aim is to facilitate a shift in culture and approach towards an embodied, holistic model by raising awareness of the problems and supporting curiosity.

Additionally, we want to create safe and trauma-informed spaces for embodied learning and facilitation, where individuality, divergence, and innovation are valued, celebrated, and encouraged.

We believe that exploration, discovery, and creativity should be the foundational values in these spaces. We also acknowledge that making mistakes is a natural part of the learning process, and that intuition is considered an essential point of reference. Finally, we believe that gut instinct should have the final say in decision-making.

---

[8] https://www.ted.com/talks/sir_ken_robinson_do_schools_kill_creativity

Embodied Education – The Model

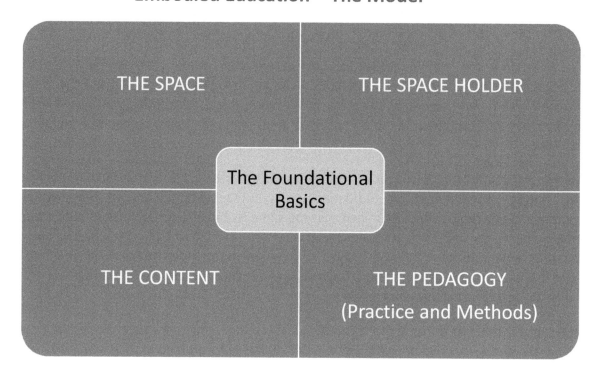

How to use this Manual

Having now viewed a visual representation of the model of an Embodied Education (see *The Model* page) you can see that it is made up of five areas:

The Foundational Basics
The Space
The Space Holder
The Content
The Pedagogy (Practice and Methods)

Within each of the five areas are sections which include:

- Topics
- Discussion
- Future Visioning and 'Try This' exercises which provide prompts and practices for you to explore.

We called this a manual instead of a book as it offers information and guidance on how to create trauma-informed, safe, professional and accountable learning and sharing spaces and environments. However, there is a workbook and collaborative aspect of it as we wanted you to draw on your own experience and truth – and offer you an opportunity for personal growth and healing via self-reflection should that be useful to you.

Ideally you will read this manual start to finish in order – however, you are welcome to jump to different areas and other sections if you are drawn to a particular topic. If that is the case, we would request that before you do this, read *The Foundational Basics* section of the manual, which offers key and core information for creating safe, trauma-informed and nervous system friendly environments.

The manual is structured to provide information on a specific topic, followed by prompts that encourage you to reflect on your own perspectives and consider how you can apply what you've learned. There are practices to support embodiment for you to do yourself and we have included additional information, resources and references in the *Further Exploration: Embodied Education* page at the back of this manual.

It is likely that you may need to read and process the manual and its contents more than once, and also review its implementation.

It may be useful to take this manual to a discussion group, team/staff meeting, or supervision session – or even explore it with your clients, participants and students. Our intention is to open a dialogue around the existing paradigm of educational, learning/ sharing spaces and organisations. We do not have all the answers.

The approach you take to collaborate with all stakeholders who have a vested interest in the spaces operate in, and the agreements you establish to ensure safety and well-being, will be customised and distinctive to that particular setting. We have provided a range of topics for discussion, feedback, information, future outlooks, and guidelines for you to review and contemplate.

Before you Start

Reflect.

What do we carry with us as teachers, facilitators and space holders from our own schooling experience?

What do we carry with us as learners?

Our own experience of school creates a mental, emotional and physical template and schema for teaching and learning, indeed being part of any facilitated space – in any capacity – for the rest of our lives unless we fully investigate and process it. It informs how we show up as space holder, facilitator, teacher, participant or student.

Think back to your school experience. *What are your most vivid memories and feelings about the building, the teachers, your friends?*

In gathering views for this book, we asked questions of a worldwide audience via an anonymous online survey about their experience of schooling. For more information about respondents, go to the *Thanks to the Survey Respondents* page at the back of the manual. Results showed that the majority had not experienced educational or facilitated spaces as safe. A safe space can be defined as 'a place where everyone can feel comfortable about expressing their identity without fear of discrimination or attack, and a situation or place where a person can feel comfortable and secure'.[9]

In relation to schooling, one responder emphatically and clearly stated, 'I never felt safe in that situation.'

Many explained that they continue to carry trauma within their system from that time of their lives. Some descriptions mentioned that it was their 'worst life experience,'... 'degrading, inhumane' and 'something I survived'. Past experiences of spaces of facilitation, teaching and learning were associated predominately with physical and psychological stress; stomach pain 61.1%, headaches 54.8% and exhaustion 64.8%, being shamed 68.8% and holding in emotion 81.5%.

How many of these symptoms do we currently observe in the children of today when they return home from school? How often are these symptoms passed off as a bad mood, hormones, a bad day, lack of sleep, exam stress? Whilst these things need to be considered in relation to supporting health and wellbeing, ascertaining whether these symptoms are due to chronic stress and trauma caused by the educational experience and learning environment, is an enquiry to undertake – and one, we do not have the immediate answer for.

---

[9] https://www.macmillandictionary.com/dictionary/british/safe-space

The feedback we received suggested that the experiences people had in school were mostly negative and have had a lasting impact on them.

These negative patterns can be carried over into their approach to learning as adults, whether they are a student, teacher, or facilitator, in various settings like classrooms, conferences, sharing circles, or yoga classes. Even with the very best intentions, unless we consciously reflect on our own formative educational, schooling and learning experiences, it seems we can repeat what we experienced – often without any awareness of what we are doing.

Psychological theory provides evidence for this and teaches that we do indeed repeat what we don't repair. Freud talked about repetition compulsion – where individuals re-enact or (often unconsciously) find themselves in the same or similar situations, relationships, or dynamics again and again. It is thought that this phenomenon happens in attempt to bring resolution to the original trauma or stressor – to gain mastery and peace around it.[10]

It is vital then that space holders, facilitators and teachers be aware of this in themselves and also in their clients and students. Unless we consciously assess, reflect and repair our own school-based trauma and automatic patterning, consequences could range from catastrophic PTSD responses to the insidious ongoing perpetuation of toxic learning and sharing environments. If we continue to re-enact – without analysis – the traditional authoritarian model and power-over structures of teaching and learning that we experienced, we will automatically repeat this in our space holding, facilitation and teaching – even if this is not aligned with our own values.

So, before you begin reading this manual, reflect on your own values and attitudes toward teaching, facilitation, space holding, learning and education.

Start by thinking about your thinking.

What are your values?

---

[10] *Trauma and Recovery*, Judith Herman p 41-42

Values are those things that you feel are important in how you work and live. What follows is a list of values [11]. It is not exhaustive – you can add or use others.

Circle your top five work values:

1. Acceptance
2. Achievement
3. Ambition
4. Adventure
5. Bravery
6. Collaboration
7. Creativity
8. Curiosity
9. Empathy
10. Excellence
11. Fairness
12. Family
13. Friendships
14. Flexibility
15. Growth
16. Happiness
17. Hard work
18. Honesty
19. Humility
20. Innovation
21. Integrity
22. Intuition
23. Kindness
24. Knowledge
25. Leadership
26. Loyalty
27. Motivation
28. Open communication
29. Optimism
30. Passion
31. Patience
32. Popularity
33. Power
34. Professionalism
35. Punctuality

---

[11] https://ca.indeed.com/career-advice/career-development/examples-of-values

36. Quality
37. Relationships
38. Reliability
39. Respect
40. Responsibility
41. Safety
42. Security
43. Spirituality
44. Stability
45. Success
46. Tenacity
47. Time management
48. Wealth
49. Wisdom
50. Work-life balance

Now ask yourself, what is my definition and understanding of the book's key words listed below? Write your definition alongside each word:

- Body
- Creativity
- Education
- Embodiment
- Evolution
- Facilitation
- Feminine
- Instinct
- Intuition
- Learning
- Masculine
- Metacognition
- Mind
- Nervous system
- Organisation
- Power
- Relationships
- School
- Sharing
- Space Holding

- Stress
- Teaching
- Thought
- Trauma

Then ask yourself:

- *Are these definitions actually mine, or something I have inherited – been told – absorbed?*

- *How has my own personal experience of school impacted on how I define and understand these key concepts?*

- *After reflecting on this would you like to change your answers?*

Now notice your body's reactions and sensations.

If you are struggling to do this – if you don't feel anything in your body – you can try this short somatic ABC exercise to reembody and make contact with your body. It's completely normal that paying attention to and being aware of your body requires effort and practice.

ABC Exercise

A: ANCHOR – Feel your feet on the floor and bottom on the chair.

B: BREATHE – Notice your breath.

C: CONNECT – Place your hand on your stomach or heart to link mind and body.

Then consider the questions below:

- *How does your body respond to the words and ideas above?*

- *Is this different than your mind's response?*

- *Does your body's response convey a different message than what you're thinking?*

- *Are there any surprises?* Reflecting on this, *would you like to change your answers?*

Now notice your emotional reactions and response:

- *How do you emotionally respond to the words and ideas above?*

- *Is it different than your mind and body responses?*

- *Are there any connections?*

- *Does your emotional reaction tell you something different than your thoughts?*

- *Are there any surprises?*

- *Reflecting on this, would you like to change your answers?*

Finally – reflect on what this exercise revealed to you about what you are carrying with you as you move into the forum of education, facilitation and space holding.

Definitions

Before you read this content, please ensure you have read the *Before You Start* section where you are asked to define some of these words for yourself. Your own definitions and understanding may change as you move through the manual or after you have read this page. However, it can be wise and empowering to first self-reference and defer to your own responses and inner knowing. Begin by focusing on your personal experience, thoughts, and knowledge, while also maintaining a sense of curiosity and openness to making changes and adjustments.

These are our working definitions and explanations of the manual's key terms:

Body

Physical structure of a person – flesh, bone, organs – animal self.

Boundaries

Definition of where one thing ends, and the other begins, and what is ok and what isn't. Communicated, negotiated and agreed on in healthy relationships, groups and settings. Part of the foundations of safety.

Content

Anything shared – subjects, themes, message, materials, texts, ideas.

Creativity

Life's urge to give life to life – the impulse to move – which is the origin of all creation. The process of desiring, receiving and conceiving, gestating, birthing and nurturing.

Education / Learning

For us, education means learning and the process through which knowledge (information) and gnosis (inner knowing and awareness) are experienced, explored and taught. We believe that education is the key to growth and change – the joy of being and feeling fully alive.

Embodied / Embodiment

Incarnated – to give bodily form to. In, through and of the body.

Evolution

The constant that is change in process. The impulse and creative process to deconstruct, simplify and align with our truth and therefore wholeness.

Facilitation / Facilitator

Offering information, support and materials for someone or a group to make progress and find their own answers to questions.

Instinct

Inborn impulse – our natural and innate motivation, knowledge and inclination.

Intuition

Innate and direct knowing of truth without conscious reasoning.

Masculine and Feminine

Two complementary energies (electric and magnetic) and principles (yang and yin), which exist and can be balanced and unified in all humans.

Metacognition

Thinking about thinking – awareness of our own thought patterns and processes.

Mind

Place of conscious and unconscious mental processes and mental functions, which includes imagination, perception, thought, intention, memory.

Nervous system

The complex control, communication and regulatory system of the body – brain, spinal cord and nerves.

Organisation

A group of people working together, with a particular aim or purpose. Also, the structures of the organisation.

Paradigm

The current and widely accepted or conformed to framework of beliefs, values, procedures, perspectives, etc.

Pedagogy

Practices and methods for teaching, facilitation and space holding.

Power

Innate energy. A force within us which we have the ability to connect with, harness, express and create change through and with.

Relationships

Connectivity and interaction between people.

Safe

Free from threat and protected from harm.

School

A place of education and learning.

Sharing

Telling others our feelings, experiences, thoughts and beliefs.

Space Holding / Space Holder

Offering empathetic and compassionate presence through which someone can be fully heard and seen.

Stress

The body's reaction to a stressor, threat or pressure.

Teaching / Teacher

Educator who provides knowledge and subject expertise for student to critically appraise, compare and contrast with alternative perspective and views. One who encourages students to tune into inner knowing, internal guidance, intuition and gut instinct.

Thought

Cognition – the action of thinking and ideas generated within the mind.

Trauma

Anything which is too much, too soon or too quick for a person's nervous system to process.

Trauma-informed

Awareness of the widespread prevalence and impact of trauma in society. Safeguarding against re-traumatisation and vicarious trauma (secondary traumatic stress – the impact that working with those who experience trauma has on facilitators, teachers and space holders).

Dedication

For our sons, James and Archie – our greatest teachers.

Thank you, especially, for your magical minds and embodiment. Thank you for thinking 'outside of the box' – divergently and creatively. Thank you for offering us the freedom of authenticity and permission to vision alternative ways of learning and another way of both being and doing.

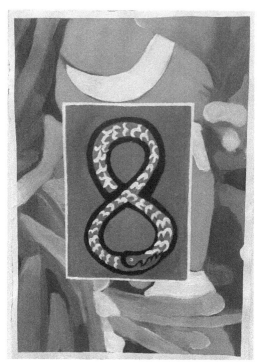

Clown Fish Party – Grase MacFarlane

www.gracemacfarlane.com

At first glance, it appears as though the number eight is slithering on top of a background that is a vomit green colour. However, upon closer inspection, it becomes clear that the "eight" is actually a snake. The snake is delicately decorated with white trimming and fine white lines that surround its internal shape. The snake is also turning into itself and resting on the softness of an outlined hand.

For anyone who doesn't know, it's the shape of the ancient ouroboros symbol – depicted in thick black lines with no regard for three-dimensional space. The flatness is exaggerated by the fine white detailing and bright green background that bleeds into the symbol and entangles it – making the shape itself and the area on which it rests, one complete piece. The ouroboros is a symbol that expresses the unity of all things, material and spiritual. This ancient symbol is held in place by bright abstract masses.

Bright orange and white take up the majority of the space with vertical and horizontal pink tentacles fighting for their place. These saturated squiggly masses are the breeding ground for the Clownfish. Bright orange and white in colour, these tropical fish are as distinct as their environment.

The Clownfish is among one of the great 'genderless' species within the animal kingdom. Having the ability to change their gender, giving them the opportunities to mate and procreate fully to their desire. They are a symbolic animal for gender unity, one that functions in harmony and grace.

This piece explores themes of symbolism of gender identity and construct. Depicting dimensions of direct flatness melding into harmony. It is a place where gender isn't a firm construct and in fact it bleeds and melds together in a colourful complete space.

Art by Sophie Skinner

Essential Understanding of the Nervous System, Stress and Trauma

There is no learning without the body.

Let us begin firstly with the body, and more specifically, the nervous system.

Understanding the nervous system and its functions, trauma, and trauma responses, is vital for effective learning, safe space holding and non-toxic wellness and spiritual communities –and in any learning environment. It is also important to recognise and understand the stress responses of the body. As an educator, facilitator, space holder or practitioner, working under the premise of 'first do no harm' is part of a well-rounded trauma-informed approach.

Knowledge of the nervous system serves to reduce fear of the body's sensations and reactivity, so that those we educate can become or remain embodied and able to access their metacognition, creativity, intuition and instinct. It's only then that we can expand and relax into our living form and recognise that our body is doing its 'job' and is keeping us safe. Then, we can begin to trust our body, come into relationship with it, understand and accept our capacity, meet our body's needs, self-soothe and self-care. The positive outcome of this is mastery, health and a deep connection with the wisdom held within our body.

When we anchor into embodiment, we incarnate, and we feel safer to be our creative and authentic self in the world. We are more able to access higher ordered thinking skills such as critical appraisal, synthesis, reasoning, comprehension, analysis and evaluation – and are less likely to be subject to abuse, manipulation and control.

Embodiment is the FOUNDATION of education, learning and collaboration. Once we are able to partner with our body, once we feel safe within it, we can access our innate gifts and independent thought and knowing.

What is the nervous system?

On the following page is a basic diagram of Stephen Porges' Polyvagal Theory of the nervous system [12].

The now widely accepted Polyvagal Theory, proposed by neuroscientist and psychologist Porges in 1994, states that there are three components and states of the autonomic nervous system which drive all emotion and behaviour. Education about these and trauma are essential for physical and mental wellbeing and creating environments where learning and safe facilitation can take place.

The base of the diagram is the *social engagement aspect of the nervous system* (ventral vagal portion). This is the place of safety, where we feel connected to others and our environment in the here and now. We are meant to live in this part of our nervous system for the majority of

---

[12] https://www.stephenporges.com/

the time. Here we are curious and here we LEARN. We rest and digest and our immune system works well.

The middle part of the diagram is where the *fight and flight* responses occur, and we also know that this area (sympathetic portion) also includes the *fawning* (also known as the people pleasing or fitting in) aspect of the nervous system. This is activated in response to stress or a perceived threat. We need some sympathetic activation in our nervous system to support action and thinking but if we spend too long in activation, we start to experience an escalation of emotions and body symptoms, anxiety, and panic (flight, moving away from the threat), anger and rage (fight, moving towards the threat aggressively) and merging with others' views and people-pleasing (fawn). Blood pressure, heartbeat and adrenaline increase, pupils dilute, we feel sweaty, digestion and immunity slow down, and we feel less connected to others. We can't fully access high order thinking skills and creativity is impaired.

Finally, if we feel we cannot escape the stress of threat we move into *freeze*, the dorsal vagal aspect of our nervous system. Here the body immobilises and collapses. We are completely overwhelmed, feel helpless, numb, depressed, and can dissociate. In freeze we also shut down heartbeat, blood pressure, body temperature, eye contact, immunity, social connection decrease, and we feel shame, feel trapped and the body prepares for death. Impactful learning cannot take place here – memory and thinking are impaired, and creativity can't be accessed. [13]

The action of the nervous system works in a way that we flow up from social engagement through flight, fight, fawn to freeze and then back down through fight, flight, fawn (deactivating) to social engagement. Sometimes in extreme threat, or in response to a stressor which feels life threatening due to a previous experience (a trauma response) we go from ventral vagal to dorsal vagal immediately. In coming out of freeze however, we will move through the fawn, flight, fight deactivation.

---

[13] For further information read Chapter 4 of Nurturing Resilience - Kathy L Kain and Stephen J Terrell

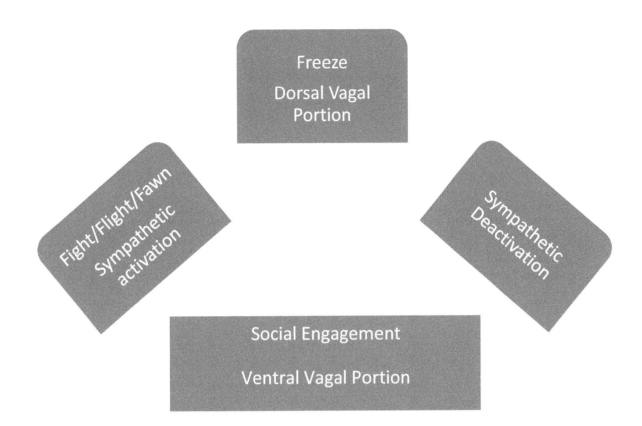

When we are in the base zone, the social engagement portion of the nervous system, we are **curious, connected and creative. Higher order and critical thinking skills are accessible,** and we are eager and willing to learn. In the middle zone, flight, we are anxious, scattered and unable to concentrate. Also in the middle zone, fight, we are frustrated, angry and aggressive. In both of these states, learning capability is impaired and behaviour can become more difficult to manage until the nervous system is regulated again. In the blue zone, freeze, cognition is offline, there is no learning or intellectual processing taking place.

How do nervous system states impact the learning environment?[14]

SAFE: Feeling Safe, open to social engagement and play
(Parasympathetic Ventral Vagal System)

Hybrid state: ventral vagal + sympathetic = play, dance, sports

MOBILIZED: Mobilized in response to a perceived threat, ready
to fight or flee
(Sympathetic Nervous system)

Hybrid state: sympathetic + dorsal vagal = freeze state of defense

IMMOBILIZED: Immobilized in response to an extreme threat,
shutdown and unable to move
(Parasympathetic Dorsal Vagal System)

Hybrid state: ventral vagal + dorsal vagal = quiet moments, intimacy

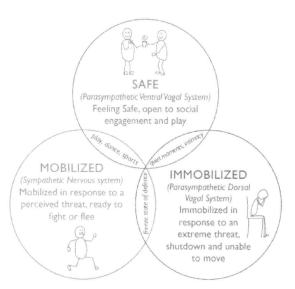

What is stress?

A stressor is *the trigger* for the activation of the body's (nervous system's sympathetic portion) stress response. The aim is to recognise the activation and our body's preferred way of responding – whether it be flight, fight, fawn, or freeze –and to stay present to it, taking steps to manage and reduce it using the *mind* AND *body*.

What is our body's preferred stress response or responses?

Knowing ourselves is powerful. Tending to our preferred stress responses is self-care. Most of us have a combination of responses and find we have different responses with different people or situations.

Are you a fighter? Do you have an explosive temper? Are you bullying, controlling, entitled, perfectionist when stressed?

Are you flight responsive? Do you experience obsessive and compulsive behaviours, anxiety, and perfectionism? Are you constantly doing and moving, worrying, and working?

Are you a fawner? Are you unable to express yourself and are you manipulated or controlled by others? Do you rarely use the word I? Are you a yes person, a people-pleaser, tending, soothing, and caring constantly for others, without standing up for your own views, needs and preferences?

---

[14] https://en.wikipedia.org/wiki/Polyvagal-theory

Are you a freezer? Do you prefer hibernating over socialising and want to hide from reality? Do you experience spacey sensations, feeling unreal, isolation, brain fog and difficulties making decisions?

So, *what are your go-to responses*? Knowing them and working with the exercises offered in the manual will support your own nervous system to regulate and bring you into the social engagement portion of the nervous system. This positively impacts the quality of the space you hold or the facilitation or education you provide.

Similarly, it will be transformative for the people you're working with if they're able to understand their responses as a way their body is trying to keep them safe. Reflect on the questions below:

How might you incorporate this nervous system education and self-awareness into your work?

How can you support those you work with to understand their nervous systems go-to responses?

What is Trauma?

Too much, too soon, too quickly.

Trauma is the reaction within the nervous system and brain, which occurs when someone does not have the capacity to stay present to it. The experience overwhelms us and takes us out of regulation.

Having a deep understanding of trauma and working as a trauma-informed facilitator or teacher is crucial. This knowledge helps both you and your students or participants to remain within a healthy emotional boundary known as the "window of tolerance". This term, coined by Dan J. Siegel, refers to the range of emotional arousal that a person can manage and cope with without becoming overwhelmed or dysregulated.

By staying within this window of tolerance, you can regulate your emotions and feel safe in your body, avoiding the risk of becoming overwhelmed or traumatised. It's worth noting that our trauma responses often follow the same pattern as our stress responses, making it even more important to have a trauma-informed approach in order to prevent triggering trauma reactions in yourself or others.

Importance of the Vagus Nerve

The vagus nerve is the primary nerve of the parasympathetic nervous system and balanced wellness and cognitive functioning. The health of this nerve (also known as tone) impacts emotional regulation and the ability to connect, trust, process information and learn[15].

This nerve is weakened by adverse childhood experiences (ACE) and trauma. These experiences are unfortunately becoming common occurrence. The higher someone's ACE score is (the more ACEs they have experienced), the longer lasting the impact in terms of health and educational outcomes[16].

Here is the list of ACES – the more someone has experienced the greater the impact on the nervous system and likelihood of trauma:

- Physical abuse
- Sexual abuse
- Verbal abuse
- Emotional neglect
- Physical neglect
- Adults with alcohol or drug issues in the home
- Adults with mental health issues in the home
- Domestic violence

---

[15] For further information: https://irenelyon.com/
[16] For further information read Chapter 6 of *Nurturing Resilience* by Kathy L Kain and Stephen J Terrell

- Adults in the home have spent time in prison.
- Parental separation

Understanding this – and how to improve the tone of the vagus nerve, whilst supporting others who are currently living in an overwhelmed nervous system state – is essential for trauma-informed, safe and effective learning environments, practitioner work and space holding[17].

What can we do to support nervous system regulation? How can we support the body to become more resilient to stress – expanding our own capacity and that of those we are working with?

It is important to know your own capacity, set a comfortable pace, and take self-responsibility when working with trauma. Working within the boundaries of your nervous system, by gradually processing experiences and information, helps you to stay regulated and within your capacity. This involves intentionally managing your exposure to stressors, pacing yourself, and prioritising the digestion and integration of content and knowledge.

By doing so, you can expand and empower your body wisdom. Expanding your capacity requires slowing down, tracking your bodily sensations (as this is how your body communicates with you), and listening to its assessments and messages. By responding supportively, you signal safety to your body, which can help to prevent dysregulation.[18]

In practical terms, supporting nervous system regulation means tending to and responding to the body's needs *first and foremost*. This means prioritising physiological needs. Things like taking rest breaks, keeping warm, cooling down, regularly hydrating, moving when the body feels it needs to, and going to the toilet as soon as you need to.

---

[17] For further information, read *Nurturing Resilience*: Kathy L Kain and Stephen J Terrell.
[18] For further information, read *In an Unspoken Voice* by Peter A Levine.

Importance of limbic resonance and coregulation

Nervous system regulation and emotional states are mutual. When we are with others physical measures such as heart rate, respiration and blood pressure change to correspond to those of the other person, particularly when looking into their eyes. The extent to which teachers and leaders are trauma-informed, regulated and balanced in their nervous system – embodied and in capacity – is the extent to which the space, children, participants and members feel safe and connected.

Basically, those leading the space set the tone, safety and effectiveness of it. The success and safety of a space depend on personal interactions, relationships, nervous system health, awareness, and accountability of facilitators. This is limbic resonance, the theory that our brain chemistry and nervous systems are harmoniously impacted or otherwise by those we are in relation with. This is outlined in the book, *A General Theory of Love*, by Lewis, Amina and Lannon. Limbic resonance involves co-regulation, a mutual internal symbiosis where the internal state of one human impacts on another and a sharing of emotional states. Trauma-informed environments take this (and the understanding of attachment theory, discussed later) very seriously.

Doing all of this for those in your space (students, participants, and those you facilitate for) is a trauma-informed practise. More about how to do this in the next section.

Future Visioning: Try This – Practising the Pause of Presence

Practise pausing and being fully there for yourself and for those you space hold, facilitate or teach. Witness yourself and them whilst meeting your own needs and encouraging them to do the same in the moment – so creating more capacity, safety and comfort – more pleasure – is the antidote to stress and trauma.

Create a pause to practise this 3-step process – **check, need and adjust** – at the start of each day, in addition to each session or lesson. By modelling this behaviour, you can help yourself and others to develop a greater sense of embodiment.

In addition, if you find you don't feel anything in your body, try the ABC exercise before you begin.

Remember – less is more. Titrate. Go slowly. Stop if you need to.

Step 1 Check

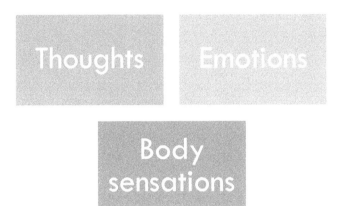

WHAT IS PRESENT FOR YOU RIGHT NOW?

Thoughts   Emotions

Body sensations

Step 2 Need

WHAT DO YOU NEED RIGHT NOW?

MIND   EMOTIONS   BODY

WHAT ONE ADJUSTMENT CAN YOU MAKE IN THIS MOMENT TO
BRING MORE PLEASURE & COMFORT INTO YOUR BODY?

What it Means to be Trauma-informed

Being trauma-informed means recognising the prevalence and impact of the behaviour, signs and symptoms of trauma on all members within the space, group, and institution –alongside understanding and being educated about stress and the nervous system, whilst avoiding possible re-traumatisation, dissociation, bypassing or adding to an individual's existing trauma and stress. Trauma-informed organisations and practitioners understand adverse childhood experiences and the impact of them, alongside other types of traumas and their impact.

These environments and facilitators also recognise, address and safeguard against vicarious trauma and secondary traumatic stress which teachers, practitioners, and space holders themselves can experience due to the impact of empathetically responding to the trauma of others. Signs of vicarious trauma include experiencing ongoing feelings and emotions in response to survivor's shares, over emotional involvement with a participant, pessimism, numbing, detachment, avoidance, distancing, isolating, reduced critical thinking, poor motivation and difficulties maintaining boundaries.

Finally, being trauma-informed means ensuring policy, procedure and practice is responsive to trauma knowledge. Practitioners, teachers, and space holders recognise their own capacity and refer to specialist trauma services and practitioners when needed. Trauma-informed approaches are for everyone, not just those with specialist training.

Main types of traumas

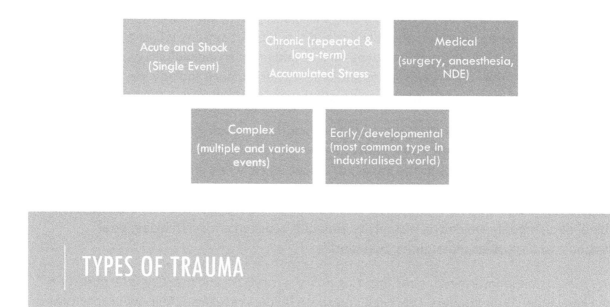

TYPES OF TRAUMA

In addition to those listed above, there are also a variety of common day-to-day experiences which can result in trauma.

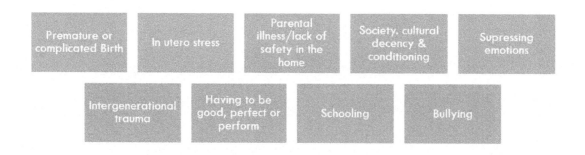

COMMON EXPERIENCES WHICH CAN BE TRAUMATIC

Impact of trauma

The physical and emotional impact of trauma can result in the following symptoms and can be the underlying cause of illness in a person who follows a 'healthy lifestyle' but still remains 'unwell.'

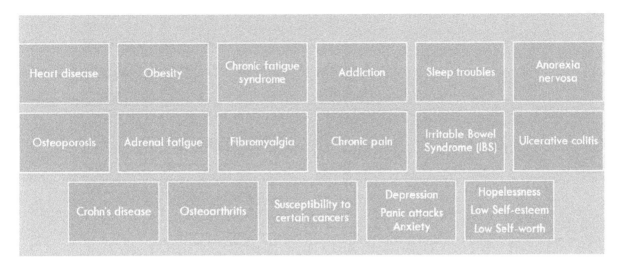

IMPACT OF TRAUMA
PHYSICAL & EMOTIONAL

The relational impact of trauma can present in the following ways and can end up with the individual feeling or being isolated, further abused or psychologically distressed.

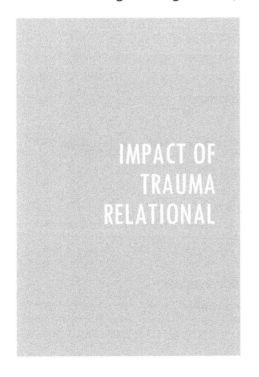

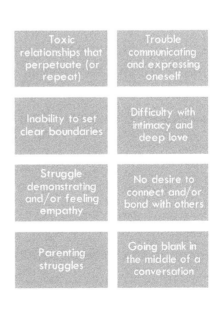

Trauma can also reduce productivity and impair creative, academic and professional outcomes.

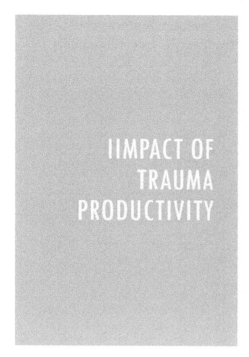

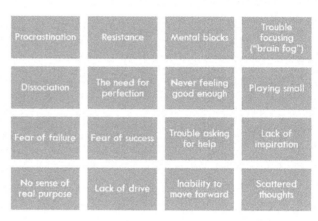

Procrastination	Resistance	Mental blocks	Trouble focusing ("brain fog")
Dissociation	The need for perfection	Never feeling good enough	Playing small
Fear of failure	Fear of success	Trouble asking for help	Lack of inspiration
No sense of real purpose	Lack of drive	Inability to move forward	Scattered thoughts

Please note that trauma may be at the root of challenges and difficulties *but it is not the role of teachers, facilitators or space holders to diagnose.* It is their role to be trauma-informed and aware.

Trauma-informed spaceholding, facilitation and teaching – alongside trauma-informed spaces, communities and institutions – take all of the above into consideration and offer a whole organisational approach which usually includes the following:

- Safety
- Recognition and acknowledgment of trauma
- Understanding trauma effects people in different ways
- A consistent whole institutional, community and staff approach
- Transparency – explicit about roles, services, timings
- Policy, procedure, risk assessment and guidance for the avoidance of retraumatisation
- Choice
- Empowerment
- Peer support
- Collaboration
- Trustworthiness
- Cultural, historical, gender, diversity sensitivity and responsiveness
- Contingency and referral routes to specialist trauma treatments
- Clear boundaries
- Respectful environment

- Sensory, calming, nervous system friendly environments

The space will also have policy and procedures, alongside risk assessments, in place in response to stress and trauma, Staff will be trained in how to reduce the risk of vicarious trauma by taking actions such as:

- Self reflection
- Supervision and debriefing
- Self care
- Wellness schedule
- Work-life balance assessment
- Coaching and planning of realistic intentions
- Coaching and mentoring clients, students and participants to help themselves – not saving
- Regular breaks
- Social network
- Peer support
- Individual therapeutic care and ongoing training

Future Visioning: Try This – Support the Resolution

The following five topics are the foundations of trauma-informed practise, from which the resolution of trauma and stress can flow. In individual facilitation, space holding and teaching, it is useful to weave all of these components into your work: nervous system and trauma education; safe support and connection to you as the practitioner, the group and the client to themselves; developing mastery not fear of physiology and embracing embodiment and sensation; staying present to big feelings – physical and emotional – all whilst employing somatic and nervous system tools to increase capacity, regulation and the window of tolerance.

All these components need to be consistently applied and embedded within policy, procedure and staff training programmes for an organisation or community to ensure it is a trauma-informed environment.

HOW TO RESOLVE TRAUMA & STRESS

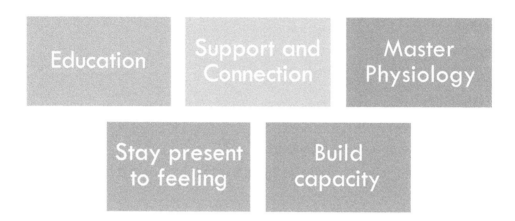

Reflect personally and take this to your next supervision, community or staff meeting to open up discussion.

More information, exercises and suggestions on all of these issues is included throughout the manual.

Basic Wellness – Essential Bodily Needs

Why is an awareness of the body so important when preparing, planning and facilitating education?

One purpose of education is to support motivation to create and learn, develop and achieve your full potential. A well-known theory of potential is Maslow's Motivational Hierarchy of Needs[19] which establishes the basic needs for self–actualisation. The first step or basic foundation is the *Physiological* needs of the body such as food water, fresh air and water. See also Kim Golding's pyramid and assessment grid for meeting the needs for traumatised children[20] in which she emphasises the need for comfort and co-regulation, empathy and reflection, exploring trauma and mourning losses.

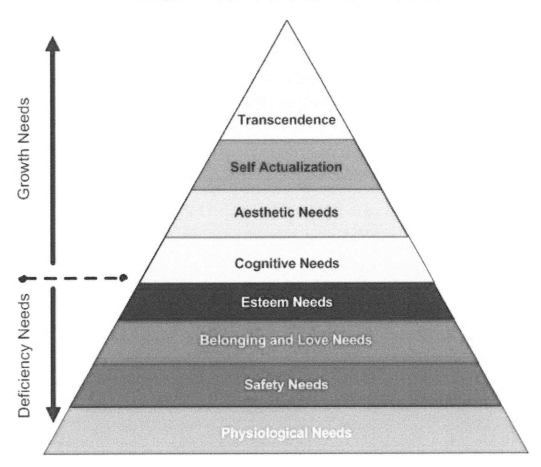

MASLOW'S MOTIVATION MODEL

---

[19] https://commons.wikimedia.org/wiki/File:Expanded_Maslow%27s_Needs.webp
[20] https://kimsgolding.co.uk/resources/models/meeting -the-therapeutic-needs-of-traumatized-children/

However (as is the case in most schools), not being able to eat when we are hungry, drink when we are thirsty, use the toilet when we need to, walk around and get fresh air when we need to, move and wear clothes to keep warm or cool, means that – according to Maslow's hierarchy of needs – we cannot access safety, connection, esteem, creativity, problem solving or achievement. As one participant described in the informal questionnaire, long lasting difficulties are caused by 'not being able to take jumper off if feeling too hot, and not being able to leave lessons if subjects were distressing/triggering'.

Our feedback showed that for students and staff alike, physiological needs, rights and basic dignity were not being met within the institution of school. Far from being trauma-informed, school itself is causing long-term physiological and emotional trauma. Participants comments clearly demonstrated this. One comment stated, 'I remember having stomach aches and constipation – I would be conscious about being in the toilet 'too long' whilst being doubled up in pain' and another read 'I recall at 8 years old, desperate to go to the loo but too afraid to ask in case of a disciplinary. I wet myself on the teacher's new carpet and was made a spectacle of in front of the class'. A teacher also explained that 'being in charge of a class means you often cannot use the toilet when you need to (particularly while pregnant)'.

Unless basic physiological needs are met, we will not feel safe. We will be in survival mode – fight, flight, fawn, or freeze. In this state, no critical thinking, complex cognition or creativity can take place. Based on our findings for most participants, school was not a place where the body was safe or catered to and cared for. School trauma was the prevalent landscape.

One teacher commented that 'exhaustion, holding in emotion and headaches are all part of the job,' whilst another explained that the experience of teaching is 'inhumane' and 'the inability to leave the room for most of the day and being on show, whilst delivering lessons meant that all personal needs were subjugated to the needs of the job'. Participants described their school experiences as causing 'panic attacks', 'intimidation', 'humiliation' and 'shame'.

Organisations need to be aware and address this, as there is no learning without full embodiment. One contributor commented that there was a 'total denial of the body in school' and that as a student they were 'perceived as a brain to pour facts into'.

In addition, as we move into adulthood our body can re-enact the freeze reaction, we can experience a PTSD response in group, learning or sharing situations and so trauma informed facilitation and space holding will be aware of this and undo this patterning by creating a different leaning environment – where basic wellness is paramount.

Essential bodily needs

Here is a model to consider in supporting us to learn and explore as *well* human beings.

Foundational to the pyramid of well-being are a set of wellness factors, listed below. Trauma-informed and embodied education spaces will ensure that students and participants have these needs met where appropriate.

Physical Wellness Factors

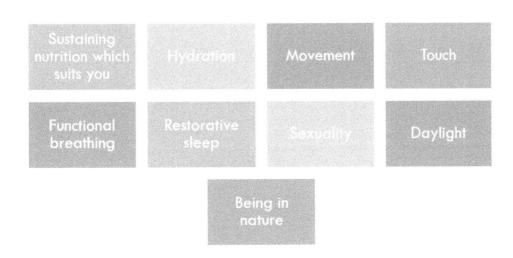

WELLNESS FACTORS — ENVIRONMENTAL, NERVOUS SYSTEM, MEANING, EMOTIONAL, CREATIVE, SOCIAL

Once wellness factors are integrated into facilitation and the space itself, then embodied mindfulness – the next step on the pyramid – can be considered.

Embodied Mindfulness

Embodied Mindfulness is being in the NOW in our mind and body – noticing, being with and in our body, and providing containment for our thoughts, feelings, body sensations and the world around us. As was explained in the *Essential Understanding of the Nervous System* section of this manual, limbic resonance and coregulation highlight the importance of the teacher, space holder and facilitator – leading the way, modelling and expressing this themselves through and in their body – thereby setting the tone of the space as embodied, contained and regulated, i.e., safe.

In embodied mindfulness the feet and pelvis are the anchors of awareness. An anchor is something which keeps us connected to the body, environment, here and now and reduces wandering thoughts, dissociation and daydreaming. Noticing the feet and pelvis *before* focusing on breath and orientating to the environment reduces the risk of dissociation and bypassing.

At the top of the pyramid is the practise of self-compassion. Attention can be turned to that once embodied mindfulness has been mastered and woven into facilitation.

Self-Compassion

Self-compassion is extending compassion to ourselves in instances of perceived inadequacy, failure, or general suffering. It is being our own best friend and parent. Kristin Neff has defined self-compassion as being composed of three main components:

1. Self-kindness (not self-judgment)
2. Common humanity (not isolation)
3. Mindfulness (not over-identification)

In embodied self-compassion, it is useful to incorporate safe self-touch to the body (e.g., stomach when fearful of conflict, heart when anxious or sad), as part of the learning and sharing environment – in addition to modelling compassionate, calm and affirming language and self-talk. Boundaries around how students and participants address each other is also important. These boundaries reduce the repetition of old learned toxic ways of interacting which were combative and bullying. Having a reflection of outward compassionate boundaries (and shared and differing views) reprogrammes our inner voice and self-talk.

There is more about all of the above, as well as suggested practises, throughout the manual.

Future Visioning: Try This – Three Steps for Prioritising Wellness

At the start of every lesson, session, circle, staff meeting, or community gathering, complete the three-step process for prioritising wellness. The aim is to make the steps – the questions and actions – routine and reflexive. This requires that everyone – practitioners and participants alike –do this consistently. It will then become embedded into the participants body and mind so that they will automatically start prioritising their own needs and supporting the regulation of their nervous system, reducing stress, undoing freeze patterns and building capacity.

Step 1: Holistic Presence to Self – Self-Referencing

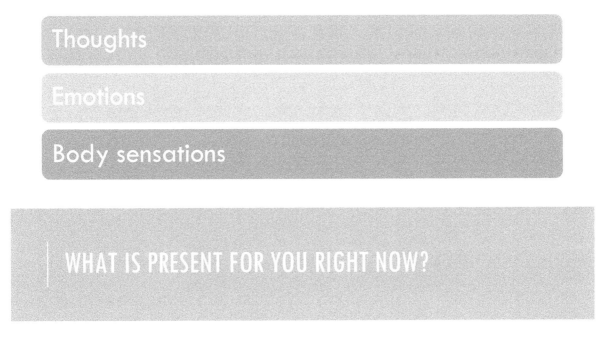

Thoughts

Emotions

Body sensations

WHAT IS PRESENT FOR YOU RIGHT NOW?

Step 2: Meeting Own Needs – Self-Parenting

MIND   EMOTIONS   BODY

WHAT DO YOU NEED RIGHT NOW?

WHAT ONE ADJUSTMENT CAN YOU MAKE IN THIS MOMENT TO
BRING MORE PLEASURE & COMFORT INTO YOUR BODY?

Body Intelligence

The mind is only one aspect of the intelligence we can access as humans. The body also carries its own intelligence. The communication between mind and body is complex with both parts constantly sending and receiving messages in a feedback loop.

Body intelligence is currently not acknowledged in education. Only 1.9% of participants described their experience of schooling as body-based, whilst 28.3% described it as 'reason-based,' 69.8% as 'controlled' and 26.4% as 'logic-based.'

Part of embodied education is acknowledging the wisdom of the body – to listen to it and learn from it. As a space holder, facilitator or teacher, encouraging and validating "body knowing" of those in your space is trauma-informed practice and strengthens and empowers the courage and confidence of your students.

Gut Instinct and The Ick

The relationship between the mind and gut is known as the gut-brain axis, a superhighway of information sharing which happens between the GI (gastrointestinal) tract and CNS (central nervous system). Gut instinct is natural and innate motivation, knowledge or inclination – an intelligence of the body which often processes and has the answer or response to a situation before the mind does. This instinct is about survival and helps us to assess and have an immediate understanding of the truth of a situation. Instinct is a mammalian superpower – a gift of our animal self, also known as interoception[21] – which communicates through inner physiological sensations and signals, such as a somatic gut response like butterflies or nausea – or outside the gut in ways that may include an increased heart rate, pain or tightness in chest.

'The ick' is a useful slang term which means to feel 'turned off' to something. The body is the ultimate lie detector. If we fool ourselves the body revolts and objects and we get 'the ick' – a sensation of disgust. If others are fooling, controlling or manipulating us we also get 'the ick'. As a facilitator, it's important to validate and support those in the space you are holding, as they tune into and express their responses. Doing so can help to strengthen their instinctual knowing and promote self-protection and inner guidance.

Excessive or long-term stress or trauma can skew gut instinct responses, dampening them or heightening them to the extent the signals are no longer an accurate response. It is therefore important to triangulate 'knowing' and intelligence – checking the mind's response alongside the intuitive and instinctive response.

---

[21] For further information read p 26-29 of *Nurturing Resilience* – Kathy L Kain and Stephen J Terrell

Impulse

Impulse is the urge the body feels to move and create – so it is a bodily creative intelligence, movement, or life flow – moving itself towards fullness and joy. Creativity is an essential aspect of embodied education and wellness, so encouraging this organic rise of movement ensures original thinking amongst those in your spaces.

Intuition

Intuition, sometimes referred to as the sixth sense, is closely related to instinct. However, how it works – how we know through it – is bespoke and unique to us individually. Sometimes we 'see', sometimes we 'feel' and know through emotions, other times we taste or hear or the intelligence just 'drops' into us – i.e., we just know. Intuition is an innate and direct knowing without conscious reasoning. Intuition and access to inner knowing can be strengthened by increasing emotional intelligence – developing a relationship with our emotions and moods. As a space holder or teacher referencing the intuitive response of those participating in the space (alongside their instinctive and logical or cognitive responses) increases confidence in decision making, cultivates creativity and autonomy and promotes inclusivity. It increases life satisfaction and wellbeing.

Future Visioning: Try This – Asking for Three Answers

Body Intelligence might not be immediately accessible as we rarely reference it in educational or learning spaces. Participants and students might not be able to feel their body or access their gut instinct, body signals and sensations in their bodies.

Trauma-informed practice ensures that the body remains part of the learning process and so asking for three answers – having three points of orientation when considering any topic – ensures that all parts of animal self (mind, emotions and body) are part of a collaborative and unified process. This helps safeguard against dissociation and bypassing and promotes holistic learning and intuitive/instinctual knowing.

Suggested questions for soliciting three answers – from mind, emotions and body. (NB the second set of questions are especially useful for younger children).

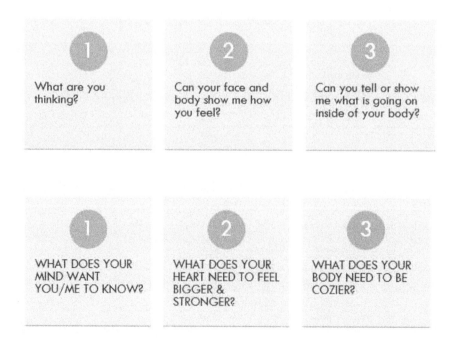

Attachment Theory

Trauma-informed, safe and embodied education makes understanding attachment theory[22] a priority.

According to attachment theory, relational skills, quality and safety are affected and informed by the quality and security of attachment between child and caregiver in early years. This is true for both space holder and participant, regardless of age.

Attachment theory was first posed by psychiatrist John Bowlby in the late 1950s following his research on the impact of child and parent separation. It suggests that babies are born with the innate need for a 'care-giving bond' – an emotional bond with their caregiver. The protective quality, sensitivity and security of this bond is determined by the tone and responsiveness of the caregiver, particularly in the first 6–24 months of life. If the caregiver is appropriately and affectionately responsive, dependable and consistent, the baby internalises safety and has a 'secure base' from which to separate from caregiver and discover the world.

A secure base offers survival and security for body and mind and is important for nervous system regulation, stress management, resilience, motivation and ability to learn. Having a secure attachment figure in threatening situations in the first three years of life especially, increases mental stability as the fear response is modulated and tempered. The quality of early attachment determines wellbeing and ability to discern those who are trustworthy. Those who did not experience healthy attachment as a baby are at risk of emotional, social and learning problems – in addition to mood disorders, poor self-regulation and the risk of abuse and self-harm.

According to this theory, attachment style in adulthood is determined in early years, with there being four predominant attachment styles:

> **Secure:** *Relates without fear and is at ease with intimacy and self-sufficiency – interdependent.*
>
> **Anxious and preoccupied:** *Fears separation and autonomy – dependent and clingy – co-dependent.*
>
> **Avoidant and dismissive**: *Fears intimacy – distant and closed – hyper independent.*
>
> **Avoidant and fearful**: *Fears both autonomy and intimacy – relationships = pain.*

Attachment styles impact how a leader leads, and also how a space holder, teacher or facilitator relates to those in their space. The quality of coregulation is also impacted by attachment style. It is important therefore, for trauma-informed and safe space holding that facilitators and teachers recognise, assess, take responsibility and actively work with (and meet) their own attachment needs, so that they model secure attachment behaviour, limbic resonance and coregulation in their spaces whenever possible.

---

[22] For further information, read Chapter 1 of *Nurturing Resilience* by Kathy L Kain and Stephen J Terrell.

Furthermore, acknowledging, understanding and offering a taste of secure attachment for those who have insecure attachment behaviour is an important aspect of trauma-informed organisational leadership, group facilitation and space holding. Attachment theory education and training are essential to safe facilitation. The space holder, teacher or facilitator needs to provide a secure base and safe haven – staying present and responsive to feelings, supporting containment and safety when fear and big emotions arise, setting appropriate and consistent boundaries, being dependable and trustworthy, and offering praise and encouragement.

Future Visioning: Try This – Templating Secure Attachment

To ensure the best possible environment for templating secure attachment in the space you facilitate, consider implementing the following:

- Structured environment and session
- Consistent rules and expectations
- Calm responsiveness, not widely reactive
- Praise and encouragement
- Sensitivity and empathy
- Reflection and engagement
- Offer choice – but you determine what the choice is.
- Set professional boundaries – you are not 'friend', you are teacher, facilitator or space holder – this is a role.
- Ensure boundaries are upheld – so consequences are necessary and need to be communicated.
- Communicate directly, positively and clearly with nurturing facial expression, appropriate eye contact and warm tone.

Additional information about boundaries, communication and safe relating is explored later in the manual.

Safety

To be safe means to be free from danger or harm – whether physical, psychological, social, sexual, verbal, emotional, mental, spiritual or financial.

According to our survey, schooling is not safe. Only 15% of participants shared that their school experience was safe.

To create a safe space or learning environment, all of the above aspects – the relationships which occur within it, the content delivered, and the methods of facilitation – need to be free from bullying, abuse or neglect.

Safety is an absence of coercion and control. It is a state where there is no misuse or abuse of power by the leaders, space holder or any participants. This state arises when there is no forced compliance and no diminishing of the personal power or autonomy of thought, body and spiritual knowing and beliefs. Choice and autonomy are paramount.

In a safe space, participants are not financially exploited. There is a fair exchange in response to moneys paid and clear boundaries and transparency around terms and conditions. This is something for organisations to consider.

Above all, safety is created in space by clearly defined and implemented policy, procedure and risk assessment. In addition, at a community, organisation and institutional level, authoritarian structures are avoided, leadership and supervision are sound, staff attitudes and prejudices are explored and addressed as necessary, so that equality and inclusion are upheld. There will be regular appraisals of working practices and interpersonal dynamics. Peaceful conflict resolution is promoted through appropriate expectations, boundaries and negotiation. A 'culture' of safety is predominant, and safety is valued by all.

All of the above are ingredients of trauma-informed and safe learning. Every individual in the space should be engaged, play an active role in fostering safety, and is educated on safety issues. In doing, so the resilience and longevity of the community and organisation are future proofed.

These issues will be explored in more detail later in the manual.

Future Visioning: Try This – Referencing your own Felt Sense of Safety

Our felt sense is our embodied awareness – an internal bodily sense and knowing, communicated through the connectivity of body to mind. In this exercise you are referencing your body first as to what safety is. These reflective questions will help you to get in touch with your felt sense of safety and become aware of situations which your body determines are unsafe.

This can be a useful exercise to do with participants to help determine and agree on group rules, expectation and code of conduct:

- Write down a list of things that help you access a feeling of safety.

- Next *write down your felt sense of safety* – describe what safety feels like in your body. Think about the sensations of safety, e.g., no muscle tension, slower heart rate, warmth but not hot, etc.

- Start to be aware of when you do not have this felt sense and what that feels like – reflecting on why and what makes the situation, person or environment feel unsafe.

- If you don't feel anything in your body, complete the ABC exercise described earlier in this manual.

Safe Relating

A trauma-informed approach to relating and communication involves empowerment, choice, autonomy, emotional and physical safety. Confidentiality, within safeguarding boundaries, is maintained and communication is collaborative, with the participant taking the lead, whenever possible, and setting the pace.

Several participants commented at length about the negative and long-lasting impact of unsafe relating during their school years. 58.9% stated they were bullied. Descriptions included being 'emotionally abused and shamed', 'being called bad' and experiencing 'intimidation, name-calling and belittling' as both children and teachers. 64.2% described their experience of schooling as critical.

Being trauma-sensitive and creating safety in relating is actually not that different from communicating effectively. The components are similar and will be discussed in more detail as we go along.

At its core, safe relating is non-abusive, transparent and respectful. Calmness and responsiveness are the predominant tone and quality, instead of heightened emotion and reactivity. Everyone's world view and life experiences are validated and respected. Trauma, mental health and/or physical challenges are not seen as being something 'wrong' but rather something experienced – and in the case of trauma, are the result of something that happened to them.

In safe relating there is no blame. Instead, there is dignity, kindness, tolerance and patience. There is an acceptance of other perspectives and differences. Everyone is given presence and common ground is sought. Active listening is practised and when adjustments are required, adjustments are made to the behaviour rather than the person. Body language is open and matches the situation. Self-awareness and self-care are encouraged, and personal responsibility is expected.

Safe relating in communities, organisations and institutions will support feelings of belonging and positive communication which contributes to wellbeing, and growth – and ensures that all people contribute and have their contributions celebrated and recognised.

Safe relating cannot happen without boundaries – expectations of behaviour alongside methods to appraise and maintain them. Structures of power are discussed and reviewed to safeguard against authoritarianism, coercion and control. Open discussion, participant voice and external assessment are sought. Recommendations are then implemented, and education and staff training are offered around safe relating and exemplify healthy relationships.

Finally, a key component of safe relating is the transparency, integrity and responsibility of leaders and their willingness to self-reflect, appraise and adjust ethos when necessary.

Future Visioning: Try This – Referencing your own Felt Sense of Safe Relating

We all have an innate sense of what safe relating is, which is rooted in our embodied experiences. However, this sense of safety may not always align with what we have been taught about healthy relating, particularly if we have grown up in a highly reactive or abusive home or school environment.

For instance, if we grew up with shouting, swearing, volatility, sarcasm, and coercion as the norm, we may feel safe even in highly charged situations with loud emotional outbursts during conversation. On the other hand, healthy relating, which involves calm and transparent dialogue with clear boundaries, may feel unsafe to those who are accustomed to toxic relating.

To promote healthy relating, it is important to create trauma-informed environments and facilitate modelling.

At this point, our goal is to increase your self-awareness. Additional information about trauma-informed and non-abusive communication will be offered later – but for now, let's explore the type of communication and relating that your body feels comfortable with:

- Notice when you feel at ease in a conversation or in the company of someone. Reflect on why this is. Write down how they relate. Describe the tone, pitch, volume of their voice, their body language, and the words they use.

- Notice when you feel uneasy and uncomfortable in a conversation or in the company of someone. Reflect on why this is. Note how they relate. Describe the tone, pitch, volume of their voice, their body language, and the words they use.

- If you don't feel anything in your body, do the ABC exercise described earlier in the manual.

Boundaries

Boundaries are essential for organisations, groups and spaces to be trauma-informed and safe because they are at the core of healthy relationships. In addition, modelling appropriate boundaries supports others in recovering from trauma as it provides a template and permission to understand and set boundaries – something which trauma may have impeded. Personal boundaries have often been violated in cases of trauma, or in the cases of neurodivergence or learning difficulty, which can be challenging to understand and define – so it is paramount for safeguarding that in spiritual, wellness and educational forums, boundaries are a key priority.

Boundaries define where one person ends, and another begins. Boundaries define a sense of self – what and who we are as individuals. They safeguard against enmeshment and co-dependency. They support us in our autonomy and sovereignty and allow us to grow in personal power – knowing that we have separate feelings, perspectives and thoughts than others, and that is healthy. Since people, organisations and groups are constantly evolving and changing, boundary setting is never a one-time event, but is an ongoing negotiated dialogue and process. Boundaries may flex and alter according to who we're with and how we're feeling that day.

Without boundaries, abuse, harm, coercion, and control are likely – so as soon as a group, class or community is formed, the first priority needs to focus on boundary discussion.

In addition, without defined boundaries, resentment, burn-out or grievance can occur – especially in smaller teams where defining roles and responsibilities will protect the longevity of the organisation and foster harmony and togetherness around the shared vision and values. Boundaries increase space satisfaction.

There are various types of boundaries to consider, including: emotional, physical, intellectual, workload, priority, time, resource, communication, sexual, spiritual and energy. The issues of safeguarding and disclosure, policy and procedure are vital in wellness, spiritual and educational forums. Clarification of all boundaries needs to be discussed at the beginning of gatherings, lessons, courses and staff meetings. Structures and routines need to be in place to ensure boundaries are adhered to. Misconduct procedures are also included to safeguard everyone in the space.

Leaders and space holders also need training to make them aware that they hold positions of power and trust – this is amplified in teaching, wellness and spiritual spaces, when knowledge, whether academic or esoteric, is being delivered. Plus, there is a risk of evangelism and closed delivery in spiritual and wellness settings. Teaching any information without the offer for critique, questioning and exploration is dogmatic and dictatorial and a violation of intellectual boundaries. Supervision, accountability and reflective practice are essential. Ongoing personal therapeutic work and development are a must. This will be discussed in more detail later.

Future Visioning: Try This – Referencing your own Felt Sense around Boundaries

As human beings, we all have a "felt sense," an embodied intuition that can guide us in setting and maintaining our boundaries. However, this intuition may not always align with what we have been taught about boundaries, especially if we have grown up in a highly abusive, enmeshed, or co-dependent home. Plus, schooling does not model or offer the opportunity for healthy boundary setting.

In some cases, individuals may have grown up in a household where over-giving, saying yes, people-pleasing, and fawning were normalised behaviours. As a result, they may have developed a sense of safety in merging with others, their views, opinions, and wants, often at the expense of their own needs and boundaries.

In such situations, setting safe and healthy boundaries, such as expressing preferences and saying no, may feel unsafe, uncomfortable, or unfamiliar. The more regulated our nervous system, the more our felt sense feels safe with appropriate boundary setting. Trauma-informed environments and facilitated modelling promote this. At this point, we aim to increase your self-awareness and awareness of the groups you facilitate in – how you facilitate and the culture of the communities and organisation you operate within. Further education around trauma-informed practises and appropriate boundaries will be offered later, but for now be curious about your own boundaries and how your body reacts to them.

- Notice when you feel at ease in a conversation or in the company of someone. *How are boundaries defined? What are they?*

- Notice when you feel uneasy and uncomfortable in a conversation or in the company of someone. *How are the boundaries defined? What are they?*

- If you don't feel anything in your body, do the ABC exercise from earlier in the manual.

Power

For safe, embodied and trauma-informed groups, facilitation power dynamics need to be addressed and analysed. Power is the authority, possession and capability to act, direct or influence self or others or events. This topic will be revisited throughout the manual.

Safe settings empower and cultivate the personal power of all.

According to what we heard via our survey; schools do not cultivate the personal power of all. Instead, they are 'competitive' 71.1%, 'goal-driven' 66%, 'controlled' 69.9%, 'critical' 64.2% and places of 'dominance' 58.5%. In relation to power dynamics in education, contributors stated, 'it is hierarchical', 'men were held up as leaders in texts and images', 'teachers using power positions – standing over us, flicking chalk, shouting', 'reflects societal power dynamics in terms of gender/age', 'males were prized over women', 'domination', 'males are dominant', and 'abuse of power, some teachers genuinely seem to despise children'.

There needs to be an assessment of power structures as well as a discussion around what power is, the different types of power and how power is shared. Power distribution is complex, as communities, organisations and schools need leadership and organisation to run safely and effectively.

In order to promote shared power and foster a sense of collaboration, it is important to move away from hierarchical or kyriarchical (systems of oppressor and oppressed) structures of power. These models rely on ranking individuals according to their perceived importance or are built around oppressive dynamics of submission and domination. Instead, we can adopt a circle structure where every individual is held accountable for their role and behaviour. This approach emphasises individual responsibility, equal participation, and shared decision-making, which can lead to a more inclusive and empowering environment.

Dr Lynne Sedgmore writes about power in her book, *Goddess Luminary Leadership Wheel: A Post-Patriarchal Paradigm*. She describes in detail the following types of healthy power: positional, resource, referent (respect and integrity), conscious privilege, expert and informal (having value in the collective). Conversely, she lists the following as unhealthy power in communities and organisations: power over (dominance), unconscious privilege and power under (acting from, for example, disempowered states such as unconscious rage or victimhood).

For all members' collective wellbeing and thriving – for interpersonal relationships to be healthy and strong – all voices need to be heard and have input into organisational policy and procedure and the distribution of power, connections, and resources. Ideas are shared, unique gifts of each individual are promoted and celebrated, and everyone has clearly defined responsibilities which contribute to the manifestation of shared community and group goals. Leaders will also all collectively agree values and vision.

Being able to express needs, make requests and follow decisions, negotiate and compromise, are hallmarks of shared power dynamics. Joint decision-making and respectful discussion are part of this too, alongside conflict procedures in place for resolution, including mediation channels when necessary. Communication barriers are bridged so inclusion and access are available – and opportunities to contribute are offered through a variety of engagement channels, e.g., in person, online, anonymously. Prejudice and discrimination are addressed, including explicit, implicit, direct and indirect, overt and convert bias.

Creating a culture of inclusivity requires engaging in challenging conversations about internal constructs of prejudice, bias, and attitudes. These conversations may involve discussing sensitive topics related to age, ableism, health status, sexism, gender identity, sexual orientation, parental status, religious beliefs and practices, ethnicity, race, class, economic status, marital status, education, privilege, elitism, and internal structures of colonialism and capitalism. While these conversations can be difficult, they are necessary to identify and address implicit biases and to create a more inclusive and equitable environment for all individuals involved. Sharing knowledge and transparency around agenda and intentions is also an aspect of safety in power. Clear communication channels are essential.

Safe and trauma-informed teaching, facilitation, and space holding involves removing authoritarian, controlling, and dictatorial power structures both internally and externally. This creates an environment that fosters and cultivates individuals who are calm, compassionate, curious, and confident. They have an internal locus of control (believe they have agency and responsibility for their life) and are able to self-reference.

Too often in educational settings, the power is automatically awarded to the teacher or facilitator because of their role. However, this does not mean that they can hold space and be present. *Having knowledge does not indicate that you can facilitate and meet the needs of the members of the group.*

Be aware of the power structures within your facilitation.

To create safe, embodied and trauma-informed environments, you must address the power dynamics in your organisations or communities. Power structures need to be assessed and discussed, leading to shared power with input and views from all members. This generates clear responsibilities and collective goals led by the leader on agreed values and vision.

The goal is to remove authoritarian and dictatorial power structures and foster confident individuals with an internal locus of control. Clear communication channels, addressing of prejudice and discrimination, and an understanding that knowledge and presence are not enough to hold space and meet the needs of group members are essential in achieving these goals.

Future Visioning: Try This – Your current understanding and relationship with power

By engaging in reflective practices and promoting curiosity and exploration, individuals and groups can work towards creating a more equitable and collaborative environment.

These enquiry questions are for you to answer individually, with the groups you facilitate or for your community or staff team to discuss together.

Consider and reflect on these questions:

- *What is power?*

- *What is the purpose pf power?*

- *What does it mean to share power?*

- *What would power shared practically look like in the group, class or space you hold or facilitate in?*

- *What is empowerment?*

Navigating the Change – What it Looks Like in Practice

It is essential that safe and appropriate boundaries are established both for yourself as the facilitator and for your students. In order to apply the principles of boundary setting, you should prioritise boundary discussions and establish clear guidelines for each type of boundary. Leaders and space holders should undergo training and ongoing personal development to become aware of their positions of power and avoid violating boundaries.

It's also important to have systems in place, such as misconduct procedures, to ensure that boundaries are respected and adhered to. Clarifying boundaries at the start of gatherings and meetings is critical, and leaders should encourage opportunities for critique, questioning, and exploration to promote healthy relationships and prevent coercion or control. In addition to promoting safety and preventing harm, boundaries can increase satisfaction and prevent burnout and resentment.

Where it is not working, these things will be happening:

- No changes to approach.
- Toilet access is restricted to certain times.
- People can't get up from seat and move around without permission.
- Clothing can't be put on or removed without permission.
- Can't hydrate without permission – and it is restricted to certain times.
- Answers from mind and logic only.
- Emotions are shamed.
- Intuition and instinctive responses ignored.
- Top down, hierarchal power structures

Where it is working, these things will be happening:

- Everyone is educated about the nervous system, trauma and attachment theory.
- Everyone knows their go-to stress responses.
- Trauma-informed approaches are embedded.
- ABC somatic exercise is practised.
- The Pause of Presence 3-step process is practiced by everyone.
- Body comfort first – free access to toilets, water, movement
- Clear boundaries are set.
- Choice.
- Answers from instinct and intuition are validated and explored.
- Shared power shared and collaborative decision making.

Art by Sophie Skinner

Systems, Policies and Procedures

Trauma-informed organisations, facilitation and spaces operate from the starting point of 'first do no harm.' This doesn't mean that mistakes won't be made or that teachers and facilitators won't sometimes misjudge situations. Instead, it means that there are systems, policies and procedures to safeguard both the facilitator and the participant, plus the community itself, against these things happening. It means that the intention of the space is to be safe.

External monitoring and regulation are also important methods of ensuring that 'no harm' takes place. Effective regulation, monitoring and inspection is not fear-based. Rather, the aim is to celebrate and share good practice, highlight what could make the practice even better, and encourage education and early intervention, adjustment and amendment.

External assessment is also vital to prevent against an abuse of power by leaders and the creation of an insular 'echo chamber' or cultish community. It is concerning that holistic, wellbeing and spiritual communities and arenas have no external regulatory body or system, so unethical conduct and worse still – sexual, emotional, psychological and financial abuse is taking place without repercussion. Lissa Rankin writes about this at length in her book *Sacred Medicine*.

It is a challenge for any leadership team or community to see its own shadow and dysfunctional patterning and dynamics, which increases the risk of behaviours and ethos which cause harm. The additional concern is that there is no professional statutory regulation of alternative, holistic or complementary treatments, spiritual or wellness 'teaching' and so these modalities and this education is being offered, legally, by some who have few qualifications and experience, some have none. If the educational or community space has unregulated and often uninsured practitioners facilitating – and if the space itself is unregulated and has no insurance, systems, policies and procedures – it, by definition, cannot be safe and is of high risk.

To create a trauma-informed institution or space that offers education or therapeutic intervention, it is essential to have a comprehensive and strict set of boundaries, including a clear set of ethics, values, and ethos. These boundaries should be made clear to all individuals who attend as students, join the community, or facilitate within the space. A code of conduct should also be established to set expectations for behaviour within the space.

Transparency is crucial to prevent harm and promote autonomous decision-making. Additionally, the institution or space should be aware of its capacity, limitations, and scope, and communicate them clearly to all individuals. A safe space prioritises autonomy and consistent referral, and decision-making should be run through ethical values and boundaries to ensure they are integrated and create a culture of trust. It is recommended to engage in reflection and enquiry both individually and within groups to ensure healthy personal and collective power.

Trauma-informed service providers and organisations will have a clear assessment, screening and disclaimer process. Those coming to the space will have a clear overview of what can and can't be offered and this supports empowered and informed choice. Trauma-informed organisations should occupy a space where the culture is trauma aware, as described earlier in the manual. This is different than a space which specifically offers trauma resolution and clinical trauma-specific interventions – which require specialist training and professional regulation. Not being explicit about this means that individuals may come into community with expectations that can't be met, or worse still, share trauma which is beyond the capacity of those holding the space to regulate and process – which causes harm. Therefore, screening is essential to ensure that the space can meet the needs of those who enter it.

To be a safe and trauma-informed spiritual or wellness community, there needs to be a safeguarding around how beliefs and ideas are shared. Those attracted to these communities may have significant emotional and psychological trauma and a poor sense of self. They are at risk of radicalisation and gaslighting – especially when individuals are not centred in their own knowing.

To create a trauma-informed space, it is important to have clear and transparent communication about the purpose and offerings of the space. This can be achieved through a mission statement, vision document, or similar document that outlines the values and ethics of the space. The space should also be open to alternative views and questions and avoid imposing a certain perception or worldview on those who enter.

Roles and systems within the space should be clearly defined and adhered to, ensuring that everyone operates within their area of expertise and remit. It is important to avoid dabbling in areas outside of one's expertise, which could result in harm. A referral policy and procedure should also be in place, with clearly defined places to signpost to in case a referral is needed. This helps to ensure that individuals receive the appropriate support and care for their specific needs.

The safeguarding of policies and procedures is critically important in trauma-informed spaces. Safeguarding is based on protecting health, wellbeing and human rights, preventing harm and empowering people to live free from harm. Safeguarding is a collective responsibility and spaces which provide any spiritual, education or wellness are accountable for safeguarding all individuals in the space. The safeguarding policy of a space will clearly define the organisation's commitment to it and make it clear of the procedure to follow.

Reducing risk is paramount for trauma-informed spaces, therefore, a health and safety policy and procedure needs to be agreed upon and implemented. Risk assessments – to control risks which assess and identify hazards, who might be harmed, evaluate the likelihood and harm of the risk, record and recommend protocol to reduce the exposure to the hazard or reduce risk for all activities – are a must, as is regular monitoring and review.

Safeguarding Policy and Procedure are integral to trauma-informed spaces. Safeguarding is based upon protecting health, wellbeing and human rights, preventing harm and empowering people to live free from harm. Safeguarding is a collective responsibility and spaces which provide any spiritual, education or wellness are accountable for safeguarding all individuals in the space. The safeguarding policy of a space will clearly define the organisation's commitment to it and make it clear of the procedure to follow.

Similarly, data protection, a legal requirement of any community, collaborative or educational space where personal information is exchanged or held is an aspect of safe organisation. Regularly appraising and revisiting data protection, policy and procedure is essential as is keeping up to date with current legislation.

Ignoring maladaptive workplace norms – bullying and violation of boundaries, values, ethos and code of conduct – increases risk, compromises safeguarding and increases nervous system dysregulation and the likelihood of trauma. Therefore, appraisal, capability and support procedures, alongside bullying, equality, diversity and inclusion policies need to be in place. Community mentorship, practitioner support and supervision, all improve safety of settings. Complaints policies and procedures also need to be written and agreed.

Embodied Education aims to integrate the body into learning spaces, and so careful consideration of the following policies and procedures are important for changing the paradigm in learning and sharing – which regulates the nervous system and promotes health and the intelligence of the body:

- Sickness
- Wellbeing
- Menstrual
- Menopause
- Trauma and Stress
- Neurodiversity and Neurodivergence
- Work/Life Balance
- Rest
- Holiday
- Team Building
- Reciprocity – Financial or other exchange

The need for addressing this was highlighted in our findings. One teacher stated, 'duties, meeting and lessons mean the day is relentless with no opportunity to relax. Food is often consumed while preparing for the next lesson or in the yard doing duties. Another participant explained, 'having heavy periods meant that I often spent that week in a lot of pain but being expected to carry on as normal'. Neurodivergent students especially struggled with lighting, temperature and smells but we've found that these were an issue for most students. As one participant summed it up, 'lights – too bright, buzzing; uniform – restrictive, uncomfortable; judged constantly by peers and teachers; timings – bells still trigger stress reaction; often tired and worried about if my body would cope with periods in extended lessons'.

Future Visioning: Try This – Bringing the BODY into policy and procedure

How can your space become body-friendly?

Look back at the Foundations section of this manual and remind yourself what the nervous system needs and what the basics of wellbeing are.

How can the systems, policies and procedures of your space integrate the body's needs?

What would be the benefits of this?

Take this discussion to your next community or staff meeting.

The Building Itself

Limbic resonance and nervous system education show that a physical environment which supports nervous system regulation and health – including structures, systems, policies and procedures which create safe structures – in turn, creates regulated leaders. Regulated leaders coregulate with staff, teachers and practitioners, who in turn, coregulate with those in their spaces. Safety has a cumulative effect, and it starts with the organisational infrastructure, the building itself, the environment and the supporting systems.

Students and teachers alike commented about 'artificial lighting,' 'no sunlight,' and being 'too cold' or 'too hot', 'disinfectant smells' – all which contribute to headaches and migraines.

Embodied education prioritises the building where the community gathers. It ensures that the building is nervous system friendly and pleasant – one that is comfortable for the body, calming, health-enhancing and supports wellbeing.

This requires diligent maintenance of the building. No leaks, no broken furniture, and especially no mould. Since we spend up to 80% of our time indoors and (in terms of schooling, in spaces where ventilation can be poor, and humidity and moisture can accumulate) mould toxicity can be catastrophic for health and the nervous system. Symptoms of mould sickness include head pressure, fatigue, digestive issues, lack of motivation, brain fog, memory problems, mood fluctuations and anxiety. These obviously impact the quality of learning which can take place. Therefore, it is in the best interest of any spaces where education takes place to be mould-free.

Catering to needs and serving the body supports educational outcomes.

A trauma-informed building that supports embodied facilitation will have all aspects of accessibility needs met. In terms of practical application, this means that ableist structures are deconstructed and replaced with new structures that everybody can use. Audits of accessibility issues should be conducted regularly.

Visual and hearing needs are met within embodied organisations and buildings, for example, via braille or raised lettering on signs, documents available in large print, symbol use when appropriate, audio information, whilst mobility requirements are met via, for example, easy parking and reach, drop off points are kept, ramps in addition to steps, lifts available, unobstructed corridors, open and wide doors and corridors and accessible toilets.

Accessibility also requires the environment to be adapted for those who are neurodivergent. The creation of a neurodivergent friendly space it in the best interests of all individuals, neurodivergent or otherwise, because adaptations of this kind are also nervous system friendly and sensory calming. Spaces of this type activate the parasympathetic nervous system, so create fertile ground for learning, creativity and curiosity to flourish.

Accessibility also requires that the environment is adapted for those who are neurodivergent. The creation of a neurodivergent-friendly space is in the best interests of all individuals, neurodivergent or not, because adaptations of this kind are also nervous system friendly and sensory calming. Spaces of this type activate the parasympathetic nervous system and create fertile ground for learning, creativity and curiosity.

Neurodivergent-friendly environments are ergonomically sound and mind-friendly spaces which incorporate the following elements:[23]

Lights are softened, there are no strong reflections, windows have blinds, and there are no bold colours or busy patterns. No strong odours are present – this includes chemicals – so cleaning products are made from natural products (such as essential oils). All noise is minimised – noise cancelling headphones are encouraged if appropriate. There are no bells, alarms, or temperature extremes. Fabrics and furnishings are made from natural materials and are neutral and un-patterned. Paintwork and walls are also muted or neutral tones – green is particularly calming. There are spaces for decompression – quiet rooms and outside green, nature-based areas. All sensory discomfort is minimised so desks, chairs, monitors, keyboards and lighting all need to be assessed. In quiet, private spaces and in public areas, furniture will include soft pads on the bottom to minimise scraping sounds. In addition, stim aids or sensory comforting resources of the individual's choosing, are actively encouraged.

An important note about toilets. Toilet trauma and phobia is widespread and so communities and schools who want to prevent re-traumatisation – or add to the trauma around toilets – will ensure that toilet environments are clean and well-maintained. Toilet paper should be soft and well-stocked. Lighting will be soft and there will be natural hand wash. Harsh chemical smells will be avoided. There will be plenty of available toilets and separate booths when possible – separated into male, female and gender neutral. Access to the toilet will be constant and toilets will be regularly checked. This is especially important as toilets can be places where people go for time out, to regulate their nervous system and have a moment of calm.

A note about uniforms – work or school. Where possible, uniforms need to be avoided so that individuals can choose clothing which suits them, their body and sensory needs. Tight clothing, ties, enforced blazers and synthetic fabrics which scratch, cause irritation or sweating are not conducive to trauma-informed or safe facilitation. Irritation and discomfort activate the sympathetic nervous system response and create frustration.

Finally, where lots of people gather in lively learning discussion or to share emotional difficulties, there can be congestion. Emotion is energy-in-motion and once it is released from a person, whether it be happiness, excitement, sadness or anger, it can congest and collect in a space. This impacts the quality and tone of the space and building. Therefore, regular energetic cleaning and maintenance of the building is essential for embodied education, learning and fresh thinking. Energetic cleansing also clears any trauma energy imprints. Opening windows, clapping in the corners of rooms, and diffusing essential oils will all move energy and clear the space.

---

[23] For more information https://www.ndti.org.uk/resources/publication/its–not-rocket-science

Future Visioning: Try This – Tracking the Wellness of the Building

Involving people with diverse needs, as a community or staff grouping assess and audit the wellness of whole building and space, referencing the ideas above. Consider how the environment impacts on all groups:

When do adjustments and changes need to be made?

- Immediately

- In the short term

- In the long term

Then ask:

- *What can I control and individually change?*

- *What can I influence?*

- *What support do I need?*

Make the changes and track their impact.

Interpersonal Dynamics

Interpersonal dynamics shape the culture and its ethos. They impact the success and bonding of the team. Healthy dynamics of this kind support the creation of a positive environment, one which is low-conflict, harmonious and trauma-informed. Community is key – interdependence and reciprocity – give and take is valued. Respect and trust are fostered, reflective and active listening is engaged, and transparency is pivotal to relating. There must be no deception or blaming.

Leadership plays the key role in interpersonal dynamics – setting the workplace norms and expectations via behaviour and role modelling. Leaders ensure that the roles of group members are clearly defined, and boundaries are explicit and implemented. A collaborative approach is nurtured, group members are publicly praised, and members' specific expertise is sought out and valued.

The more people in the space or community, the more complex interpersonal dynamics become. Leaders may need to seek professional advice or engage someone in a human resource coordinator role, alongside a crew mentorship position to maintain positive standards of interpersonal dynamics and professionalism. Leaders can't be spread so thinly that they are overwhelmed, because if they are (and their nervous system becomes dysregulated), this impacts on the team and the regulation of the space. Leaders need to understand themselves and be self-aware and reflective, be self-regulated and measured, highly motivated, build a functional and positive team, and have advanced problem solving and decision-making skills.

Interpersonal dynamics which value all aspects of wellbeing and nervous system health provide embodied education. Facilitation skills which grow healthy dynamics include listening, questioning, conflict resolution, using feedback and advanced language, and communication ability. Speaking from the 'I,' focusing on problem solving, and being empathetic help too.

Within any community – whether school, wellness or spiritual – family constellations and patterning, dysfunction and repetition can unconsciously play out, alongside attachment wounding. Awareness and honest discussion about this are vital for healthy interpersonal dynamics. The aim is to resolve the dysfunctional patterning so that interactions amongst leaders and staff, facilitators and participants is adult-to-adult ('I'm ok' and 'You're ok' by Thomas A Harris[24]) – not a child-to-adult state of domination, fawning or people-pleasing.

Spiritual and wellness communities need to be aware of potential cultish or 'high control' dynamics. Those who join the community may be vulnerable and have an underdeveloped or poor sense of self – or conversely, an inflated ego and narcissistic tendency.

---

[24] *I'm Ok, You're Ok: A practical guide to Transactional Analysis*, Thomas A Harris.

Participants in these spaces may also have an over-reliance on addiction to self-help practices or spirituality which impacts the dynamics and disembodiment, dissociation or spiritual bypassing. Interpersonal dynamics to avoid for the formation of healthy dynamics include:

- Leadership which has absolute control and is authoritarian (plus often charismatic and narcissistic)
- Extreme initiation rituals – often done in secret
- Leadership infallibility and 'special powers'
- Concealment of 'higher truths and secrets
- Denial of any truth or ideology other than that offered by leadership.
- Closed language system and 'magical' thinking
- Control over personal life of group – leadership chooses who can join
- Aggression and deception in recruitment
- Denial of own beliefs
- Unable to ask questions and critique.
- No critical thinking
- Extremism
- No forum or channel for grievances or concerns
- All content taught has to be run by the leaders
- Denial of mainstream research
- Self-doubt is encouraged.
- No external assessment or regulation
- Leadership believes they are above the law.
- Elitism
- Threats
- Outsiders vilified
- Isolation
- Group identity stronger than individual identity
- Emotional frenzy and mind-altering practices
- Zealous commitment and loyalty
- Over dependence on the group
- New members love bombed.
- Financial abuse
- Group members controlled

A board of governance, trustees or 'elders' sourced from outside the community and organisation are useful to provide transparency and safe steering of interpersonal dynamics, culture and ethos.

Future Visioning: Try This – Facilitator, Teacher or Leader Know Thyself

- Are you self-aware?
- Consider facilitating feedback on your leadership, teaching or space holding.
- This can be offered via a full 360-degree analysis anonymous questionnaire or a 10-question anonymous survey you write yourself online.

Your goal is to see if *how you think and how you perceive* matches up with how you are received and perceived in the outer world.

External Inspection

This section of the manual addresses the importance of external inspection and explains why it is an integral part of trauma-informed communities, organisations and institutions.

From the perspective of mainstream schooling and education establishments, the inspection process helps to regulate, safeguard, improve standards and ensure educational equality and opportunity – in theory. In the UK, the current Ofsted model[25] does not follow the celebratory growth model. It is more like an audit, which plays a role in checking that policies and procedures are in place. However, it is top down, and the requirements are dictated from above, with little consideration for the real environment and the people within it. Checking that a particular document or file is up to date does not mean that an organisation is safe.

To ensure effective inspection and regulation of educational institutions, it is crucial to focus on governance and leadership. However, this is not always the case in practice. During the inspection process, leadership teams may present a false facade, masking underlying issues such as bullying, fear-based leadership, and threats of consequences for non-compliance.

These threats can activate the sympathetic nervous system, triggering a response of fight, flight, fawn, or freeze, which can lead to teachers being afraid to speak out about their experiences or report issues. Therefore, an effective inspection process should prioritise creating a safe and supportive environment where teachers and staff can openly share their experiences and concerns without fear of retribution.

Ofsted may prevent or minimise serious safeguarding issues and, in terms of 'results,' improve standards – but standards of embodiment and wellbeing of staff and students are greatly diminished by the process. Fear based inspection[26] which focuses on results only and activates the freeze, immobilised, collapsed, nervous system response– does not grow a culture where true embodied flourishing, creativity and wellness thrive[27]. It doesn't work.

However, that said, at least mainstream educational establishments have some form or regulatory and external inspection process. There is at least an option of whistle blowing and complaints process and procedures.

In the wellness, spiritual, and self-development industries, there is often no external regulatory body that oversees the quality of services provided. This means that there is no official place to make a complaint if something goes wrong, other than to the police or social services. Additionally, there is no legal requirement for practitioners to hold any specific qualifications or undergo external inspections to ensure the safety and efficacy of their work. This lack of regulation can make it difficult for individuals to know which practitioners to trust and can lead to instances of harm or abuse going unnoticed or unaddressed.

---

[25] https://www.gov.uk/government/publications/education-inspection-framework

[26] https://www.theguardian.com/education/2021/nov/19/ofsted-should-do–a–little-introspection

[27] https://www.sec-ed.co.uk/blog/ofsted-and-its-culture-of-fear/

Consequently, safety is inevitably compromised, as financial extortion and various types of abuse can occur, as well as gaslighting, brainwashing and cultish manipulation. The shadow of and behaviour within these communities can run amok without external analysis and review. The shadow is the aspect of self or organisational or community structures or relationships which is unconscious, rejected or repressed. Unless the shadow behaviours or practices being discussed are amended, toxic patterns, drama, scandal or abase can thrive. Toxic positivity, spiritual bypassing, guru and cult dynamics, misconduct, sexual abuse, fraudulent behaviour, conspiracy thoughts, white privilege and racism, cultural appropriation, colonisation, and brainwashing are all examples.

Future Visioning: Try This – Facilitating Community Voice – SWOT analysis.

- Consider taking a snapshot of the views of ALL members of the space – students, space holders, and staff. This could be sent out via an anonymous online questionnaire focusing on the strengths, weaknesses, and opportunities/threats in the building and space.
- Take this discussion to your next community or staff meeting.
- Notice your responses to the comments or suggestions which trigger you or critique current practice.
- Consider taking external advice on how to address these issues. If you are reluctant to take advice or have external eyes on the results of the community voice, that is a red flag.

Referral Pathways

As was discussed at the start of this section, knowing the scope, parameters and capacity of the community and organisation – of the space and what it provides, setting boundaries and then honouring them – are the hallmarks of trauma-informed spaces.

Referral routes are offered when the level of support required cannot be offered by the organisation and facilitators – or when learning provision does not meet the needs of the students. So, knowing when, how and where to refer is essential. Referral is needed when:

- The needs of the participant are beyond the capacity and skill set of the practitioner.
- The organisation does not specialise in the participant's need.
- There is a breakdown in the relationship between participant and space holder.
- There is a conflict of interest, e.g., friendship or family ties.
- The practitioner or space is at maximum capacity.

In the context of spiritual and wellness communities, it is essential to prioritise the safety and well-being of individuals who may have acute trauma or mental health needs. Referring such individuals to appropriate professionals or services is not only a matter of ethical responsibility but also an important aspect of safeguarding. As is ensuring that medical assessment and treatment be sought for physical ailments. This is non-negotiable for life-threatening conditions and ailments. Holistic therapies are complementary and medical and mental health professionals need to be consulted before treatments take place. Advisory services and signposting pathways for people to self-refer would also be useful.

Safeguarding policies and procedures need to be put in place with a named person. Referrals should be made to social care, mental health services, police, GP and any other service when the person is at risk to themselves or others. This applies to participants, those in the space and the space holders themselves.

It is useful for every organisation to have a referral and signposting list of trusted routes, people and organisations for practitioners and participants in the space which include local telephone numbers, contact names and addresses of:

- Police
- Social care
- GP practices
- Hospitals
- Mental health services
- Alternative education provision, e.g., schools
- Counsellors and psychotherapists
- Trauma specialists
- Cancer or other health charities, e.g., Marie Curie or Macmillan Cancer Support

- Mental health charities, e.g., Mind
- Domestic abuse services
- Samaritans
- Childline
- NSPCC
- Food banks
- Specialist charities according to the demographic of the organisation
- Tutors
- Holistic therapists

Future Visioning: Try This – Your Referral Routes

1. Assess and update your Safeguarding and Referral policies and procedures.

2. Create an updated referral list with local numbers, names and addresses.

3. Create an up-to-date signposting file of reputable and recommended people, organisations and charities.

Navigating the Change – What it Looks Like in Practice

It's important to prioritise the safety and well-being of all individuals involved. Provide regular training and resources for staff on trauma-informed practices. Offer a safe and confidential reporting system for students and staff to report incidents and have clear protocols for responding to incidents and supporting those affected.

Be transparent in communication and decision-making. Have open and regular communication with students and parents. Involve students and parents in decision-making processes and have clear guidelines for decision-making processes.

Be transparent about what can and cannot be offered to individuals entering the space. Provide clear information about services and support, have a clear and accessible complaints process, and have clear boundaries for what services can and cannot be provided.

Where it is not working, these things will be happening:

- No policies are in place for wellbeing, menstrual or menopause leave or trauma-informed practice
- Leadership has no accountability
- Fear-based external inspection
- No referral pathways

Where it is working, these things will be happening:

- Policies are in place for wellbeing, menstrual or menopause leave or trauma-informed practice.
- Environmental audit – sensory friendly adjustments and adaptations are in place
- Leadership supervision
- Affirming and coaching-based external inspection
- Clear referral routes

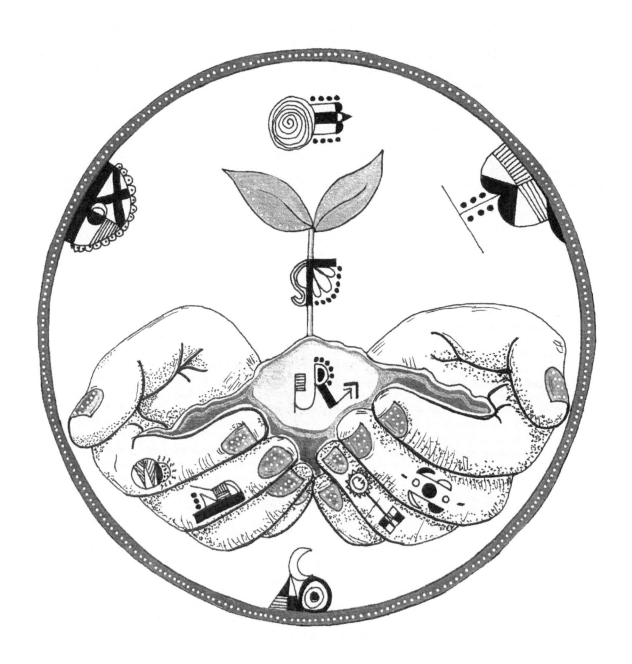

Art by Sophie Skinner

Do as I do Future Visioning: Try This – Walk the Talk Reflection Task

Congruency, behaving in alignment with what is taught or expected and integrity – behaving in an honest and ethical way both publicly and privately – even behind closed doors. These are important aspects of solid and safe facilitation, space holding and leadership. Walking the talk – taking responsibility, being solution-focused and leading by example – modelling desired outcomes and behaviour which offers a visual demonstration of 'do as an I' (and someone actually practising what they preach) creates a culture of accountability, growth and sovereignty. The space holder is trusted to keep those in the space safe and protected.

The key is to demonstrate and uphold the behaviours that you and the organisation expect. Often this is not the case, as in the example where a teacher asks a student not to raise their voice but then then shouts at students to 'discipline' them. Or consider the teacher that sanctions a student for submitting homework late but always turns up late for lessons or does not actually mark the work and misses assessment feedback deadlines set by the leadership team.

The findings show that effective teachers: 'listen', 'form relationships with students so they feel safe', 'are willing to go the extra mile', 'are willing to get to know your strengths and value them, 'respects and connects', 'has humility and high expectations', 'understands neurodiversity and different methods of thinking and perceiving', 'love their subject matter, want to expand the students view and strengthen the students sense of self value', 'can empathise', 'can read the room', 'encourages', 'encourages learning as a collaborative process rather than indoctrination', 'are self-disciplined', 'fair' and 'consistent'.

Do as I do and walking the talk for the space holder means taking responsibility for their embodiment – their nervous system, physical and mental wellbeing – in addition to their thinking and actual facilitation process. The more embodied (regulated and nervous system aware) the space holder, the more those in the space will be embodied. This is limbic resonance. The nervous system of those in the group cannot be fooled. Telling the group to relax when we are not relaxed as teachers, does not work. *Do as I do* is about the space holder fully embodying the physical and nervous system state, they want the group and community to embody. If we want those in our spaces to feel calm, easeful and safe we need to embody it ourselves first – so they 'do as I do.'

Facilitators are often surprised at the positive reaction they receive from their students when they show or express a vulnerability. For example, telling students that they have a headache and need the noise level to be low, or even simply sharing how they are feeling that day has a positive impact and more often than not, students respond empathetically and sensitively. It makes teachers appear 'more human' and relatable, plus it models authenticity and honesty.

If we want those in our spaces and communities to be authentic and transparent, we need to be authentic and transparent ourselves as leaders of the space. Workplace norms of wellbeing, stress and safety are set according to the behaviour of those in leadership. If the space holder does not implement policy, procedure and boundaries but tells everyone else that they should, the credibility of the expectation is compromised, and maladaptive norms will set in. If the space holder acts only in self-interest, are inconsistent, are not present, display passive-aggressive tendency, demonstrate favouritism and are unreliable (all maladaptive workplace norms) then this will be copied by those in the spaces. Eventually those students or community members who have integrity will leave.

To be a leader or space holder does not mean you have to be 'strong' all of the time or never show emotion or vulnerability. To clarify, "do as I do" leadership and space holding means modelling the behaviour and attitudes that you want others to exhibit. This involves being authentic, honest, self-aware, and reflective while also being accountable for your own needs. It is about showing up and being present for others, empathising with them, actively listening to them, offering praise and support, building rapport, and nurturing a sense of connection and community within the space. This kind of leadership emphasises collaboration, mutual respect, and a willingness to learn and grow together.

Do as I do leadership is process-oriented and person-centred – consistent in the application of policy and procedure and also in the presentation and behaviour of the leader. There is no pedestal for do as I do leaders – they create a circular structure in the space – they lead by example and are somatically real. This is even more essential in spiritual and wellness communities and where money is being exchanged, as many who come into the space are vulnerable and at risk.

Sharing your authentic self, speaking up, expressing how you feel or sharing a point of view is not without its challenges, especially in educational settings. The empowerment to do this comes down to the space, the space holder and the culture that is created.

The key point of this section is that the health and wellbeing of the space holder determines the health and wellbeing of the group – so self-care is paramount. The space holder/leader need to 'be the change' they want to see – so working through personal issues and growth points (alongside implementing and undertaking all practises that are taught) before supporting others in their journey, is at the core of credible mentorship and space leading. They follow their own teachings, utilise all wellbeing tools and do what they say they will do. They know and embody their capacity and capabilities.

Here are some reflection questions to determine if the actions you personally follow as a teacher or space holder – or collectively follow as a community – support you to 'walk the talk' and foster a culture of 'do as I do.'

1. *Do your own behaviours or those of the community align with the values, beliefs and ideas being taught? If not, why?*

2. *Do you and the community consistently model the change of behaviour you want to see? If not, why?*

3. *Is communication seamless and transparent to all of those in the space and community? How could it be improved?*

4. *Where there are inconsistencies in how you and the community implement boundaries ask why this is?*

Red Flags

Red flags are behaviours, actions and beliefs which indicate that there needs to be a moment of pause and assessment to see if the concern being raised is widespread and to decide if adaptations are needed.

Red flags in organisations and learning spaces include abuse, controlling and authoritarian style leadership, and no space for discussion and exploration of alternative ideas and viewpoints.

Red flags in wellness and spiritual communities, space holding, and facilitation are more complex and numerous. Lissa Rankin writes in her book *Sacred Medicine*[28] that when researching wellness, psychology, yoga and spirituality forums she found more shadow than in conventional medicine. She writes at length about space holders and teachers advocating and facilitating bliss hunting, blind compassion and spiritual bypassing – all of which support dissociation and impede feeling. These are red flags as the space holder in these instances is not facilitating embodied education or trauma-informed practices.

Other red flags in these forums include a teacher, facilitator or space holder or community space that:

- Teach that an individual is defective, bad, broken, or needs to be cured
- 'Save'
- Judge
- Deny
- 'Tell'
- Are fanatical
- Are evangelical about the method, modality or teaching they are offering
- Lack self-awareness or the ability to reflect
- Lack self-responsibility for own triggers and reactivity
- Create dependency – an ongoing 'need for them' or to attend the space or class
- Pretend
- Create an echo chamber
- Have mental health challenges which they do not take responsibility for

When encountering red flags, it is always essential to consider what your role was in how a student responded. What conditioning did you bring to the environment? Was the space safe? Did you seek permissions for individuals to share a triggering experience and was the space set up to support them after they shared? Were you denying their experience or trying to save them?

---

28 *Sacred Medicine: A Doctor's Quest to Unravel the Mysteries of Healing*, Lissa Rankin

When managing these scenarios, the use of choices is powerful as choice enables the student to remain in control, which removes any 'power over.'

Future Visioning: Try This – Is Exploration Welcome?

1. Reflect on how you react to someone asking questions about you or your communities' teaching, beliefs, methods and modalities.

2. Is curiosity, exploration and critique welcome? If yes, *how is this facilitated?* If no, *why is that?*

Responsibility

The responsibilities of space, educational and organisational leadership are many. The space holder and facilitator primarily have responsibility for ensuring the safety of the space and safeguarding all who are in it.

Knowing self – our capacity, capability, specialism and skillset – is essential and needs to be consistently referenced. Remaining focused on the experience of the students and participants, prioritising attachment and ensuring there is no bullying or exclusion – making sure that playground dynamics are not re-enacted – all are the responsibility of the space holder and leader of the community. The space holder, teacher, facilitator is the 'adults' from which everyone co-regulates and looks to for guidance.

The space holder has the responsibility of leadership, mentorship and being a role model. They are the 'elder' and 'container' of the space and all it entails. They evoke ancient ways of power like a big tree from which the shoots of the next generation bloom and grow. They recognise that the tone they set impacts the tone of the collective.

In addition, the responsibility of the space holder includes maintaining a physically clean and safe environment, as well as creating a space that is conducive to a regulated nervous system and positive energetic flow. This means no bypassing and dissociation. The space holder tracks the fight, flight, freeze and fawn reactions of group members and adapts processes accordingly. The space holder is therefore self responsible – manages their own triggers, has regular supervision, has referral and sign-posting avenues in place and uses them, when necessary. They know the depth of the space they can hold; they do not dissociate or 'check out' themselves, they have strategies and resources to ensure this does not happen – and they hold themselves accountable for the space.

To successfully maintain a safe space, you need to get to know your students, understand them, and build relationships with them.

Traditionally, in learning environments, the word rapport means 'a close and harmonious relationship in which the people or groups concerned understand each other's feelings or ideas and communicate well.' Therefore, we want to build rapport with our students.

The space holder is responsible for the power dynamics of the group. He or she safeguards the personal power of the group and shares power within the group whenever possible. The facilitator is aware of the potential for being pedestalled as a guru – and the risk of 'cult dynamics' (especially in wellness and spiritual forums) and actively ensures systems and reflective procedures of a board of trustees or inspection process is in place to ensure they don't happen.

In a classroom this also requires that teachers manage the other students' behaviour and interactions which is why there commonly is a set of classroom rules or expectations. Other environments may have a code of conduct or set of expectations that the group has read and agreed to.

In an organisation, leaders take responsibility for being balanced, fair, regulated, measured and self-responsible. They have compassionate boundaries and offer mentorship. They fear less, react less and judge less. They are responsible for ensuring ethical money transactions.

In non-educational spaces where adults assemble, space holders and facilitators recognise that there is an inevitable projection onto them of the formative educational experience and parenting experience of those in the space. They handle these 'teacher' and 'parent' projections and transference skilfully. Through self-awareness, the trauma-informed space holder manages group projections and attachment wounding – creating a safe container. They continue to work through their own issues and model ongoing personal and professional development.

They recognise that how they were taught in school (or had space held for them) determines how they teach or hold space – until they make this unconscious patterning conscious and consciously choose how to teach and hold space.

The space holder is responsible for preparation and planning, whilst also allowing for flexibility and adaptation to the group through active listening and observation. They honour the groups' wishes whenever possible. The space holder is responsible for the code of conduct, behaviour expectations, boundaries of the space and those within it. They expertly keep to time and schedules have sound time management skills.

As a teacher, plan with students in mind. Sit with a picture of the class during preparation time and be honest about what the group needs. Ask questions like:

> *Will they be able to access this work?*

> *Will they be engaged?*

Space holders are responsible for their own self-care (to prevent caregiver fatigue and burnout) and should keep their energy clean and buoyant through energy practices. They keep themselves safe and do not allow unsolicited advice or allow anyone to 'sound off' or emotionally dump on them. They are reflective practitioners but only allow reflections from others when requested and in an appropriate manner. Feedback is collected in a rigorous, but safe and contained way – via a whole group 'snapshot' e.g., anonymous questionnaire. The space holder remembers that no one is 'entitled' to them – no one owns them or is automatically given access to their presence or energy. They have boundaries around this. They also foster a culture of autonomy and self-responsibility for all group members – there are no co-dependent dynamics, enmeshment or 'saving.' The space holder has boundaries to protect their own inner child. Empathy and compassion for the group can only be accessed only when appropriate boundaries and expectations are met.

Future Visioning: Try This – Responsibility

- Reflect on what responsibility means to you.

- *How has responsibility been modelled to you?*

- *Are there any areas of space holding where you are not accepting responsibility? If so, why?*

Supervision

Supervision within an embodied organisation offers teachers, space holders and facilitators a safe and contained space to reflect on their work and explore triggers and challenges, in a non-judgemental way. Reflective practice could be an aspect of this and allows for a deepening of it as another person (ideally a mentor – someone who has walked the path of teacher or space holder), supports the individual to critique their own practice in a compassionate and helpful way to enable growth, adaptation and learning.

Supervision and reflective practice increase the effectiveness of teaching and space holding as it allows for the entirety of a person – all emotions and concerns — to enter into the workplace, be addressed, supported and resolved. In doing so, nervous system regulation ensues which creates a more positive working environment.

Supervision and reflective spaces support self-regulation as they provide a space for untangling thoughts and stress, and create coherence in the nervous system. This allows the leaders of the spaces to coregulate with the supervisor or mentor and for the space holder themselves to receive nurturance and support – filling up their cup. Supervision can safeguard against compassion or caregiver fatigue, exhaustion and burnout – if there is a coaching element which supports perspective taking and where the wellbeing of the space holder is addressed and planned for in a concrete and constructive way.

Supervision is vital in wellness, spiritual and educational spaces to support against vicarious trauma and projection. Anyone who empathetically engages with trauma survivors needs a space to 'off load,' process and integrate their reactions to the trauma, especially if the story has retriggered a trauma response in them.

Projection happens when we displace our 'discomfort and 'unacceptable' or difficult to acknowledge feelings onto another person. So, if a teacher has an especially strong or disproportional reaction to a student's behaviour they may be projecting. In wellness or spiritual arenas, projection might happen when facilitators or space holders want to protect their self-image. Projection can also be a pathway to examining insecurities or unhelpful beliefs. In supervision, projection can be assessed and worked through. Ascertaining where boundaries need to be set is vital for responding to projection.

Finally, supervision helps prevent the abuse of power and authoritarian control. A facilitator, leader or teacher who is able to thoroughly assess and face their internal struggles and insecurities will be less inclined to misuse the power they inevitably hold as someone in a position of authority and trust.

Depending on the setup of your workspace, you may find support and supervision through:

- Your line manager
- A friend
- Others in a similar role
- The welfare teams.
- Someone outside to offer a different perspective.

Many schools and colleges are now using a student support team to support their staff. You can book appointments and discuss how you are feeling, receive support. The key to the success here is building a culture where staff feel empowered to attend rather than judge.

Future Visioning: Try This – Supervision

Do you have supervision in place? If not, *why not – and where can you access this?*

How to Relate

Relating and communication is a reciprocal process of give and take – where information is exchanged, received and responded to. Effective relating is equal, without any one person dominating.

Following the premise of first do no harm, as explained earlier, understanding attachment theory is vital. As is reminding yourself of limbic resonance and coregulating. Alongside that, educating the community or receiving training in effective communication is also important.

Effective communication can be impeded by stress and heightened emotions, poor focus and negative body language. Approximately 55% of communication happens through body language – 38% through paraverbal skills (how the voice is used) – and only 7% through the words which are said, so getting educated about what makes communication effective is vital.

Engaging appropriate eye contact (according to needs and cultural background of the person in the space) is useful, alongside supportive, gentle hand gestures, natural facial expression, open posture, clarity of voice, appropriate volume, gentle tone, even pitch. These are all effective paraverbal skills. Touch is inappropriate without consent and personal space needs to be observed. Empathy and non-abusive approaches are key.

Focusing on the speaker whilst they talk and engaging active listening skills creates safer space – as does avoiding interruption, reflecting back to check understanding, and showing a genuine interest in what is being said. Avoiding judgement and paraphrasing creates empathy and connection.

Pausing, feeling the body and taking a conscious breath – and requesting time out if needed during conflict – maintains attachment and supports connection too. When miscommunication or mistakes happen, owning your part and making repairs is part of trauma-informed facilitation space holding. Apologising for your part, appreciating the impact, and offering an adjustment affirms mutual respect and maintains attachment and connection. Keeping the ego in check is important. Wanting to be right at all costs does not create mutual and healthy relating. Exploration of viewpoints and genuinely trying to see the other person's view does.

As mentioned before, safety is achieved through establishing proper boundaries. It is a challenging task, and it becomes nearly impossible to simultaneously be a friend, space holder, or teacher without appropriate boundaries, particularly in therapeutic, spiritual, or wellness contexts. It is crucial to define boundaries regarding expectations, the scope of the relationship, intentions, and other related parameters. This requires maturity and the ability to detach from repeating familiar dynamics from our family or childhood experiences.

Facilitating content via a non-fear-based dialogue is a trauma-informed approach. Creating narratives of fear does not support healthy relating.

Staying focused on the world view, belief system and language system of those in the space, filtering content through their lens and life experiences, has the greatest impact. Listening to feedback, amending and adapting as needed, and knowing when to pull back and refer also has the best outcomes safety wise for relating.

It is crucial to recognise and honour our own capacity as space holders. Establishing healthy boundaries – such as taking regular breaks, seeking assistance in resolving escalating conflicts, and mediating a resolution – are essential for creating a safe environment. If someone in the space is generating significant conflict, it is necessary to ask them to leave in order to maintain safety.

Resolving conflicts through collaboration and compromise is the most effective approach. This involves having a neutral party hold the space for both conflicting parties to be heard and working towards finding a mutually acceptable compromise. On the other hand, engaging in competition, where one individual seeks to be right or "win" without considering the impact on others – as well as avoiding or suppressing conflict, or accommodating by giving in – does not promote safety or trauma-informed relating.

It is important to engage in reflective thinking before speaking. Avoid reaching a point of heightened activation where automatic responses and conditioned patterns take over, leading to words that are disconnected from the present moment.

Always be mindful and present in your communication, ensuring that your words are rooted in the current context rather than driven by ingrained patterns or conditioning. By doing so, you can maintain clarity and authenticity in your expressions.

In schools, behaviour systems have moved on from "stop talking" to a more person-centred and blameless approach, adopting phrases such as, "I can see that you are excited about the work, and I need no more talking at present so that I can teach the rest of the content for you to consider." Always avoid using other participants as leverage, an example being "you are stopping others learning". This is shaming and undermines group relationships.

Establish clear boundaries and expectations from the start. Share these with the group so they are aware. If appropriate, ask the members to write their own boundaries and expectations. This builds a sense of ownership and collaboration from the start, and it also helps to build rapport.

Future Visioning: Try This – Conflict Resolution

What is your relationship with conflict?

Does the space you hold allow space for conflict to arise and offer a pathway for resolution?

Does the community or institution have policy and procedures in place for conflict resolution and mediation?

Navigating the Change – What it Looks Like in Practice

As a facilitator, you can create a safe and effective communication environment by understanding the principles of attachment theory and practicing effective communication skills – engaging appropriate eye contact, active listening, avoiding interruption, and paraphrasing. Boundary setting is also crucial in maintaining a safe environment, as is taking regular breaks and referring conflicts to mediation. The facilitator should also be mindful of their own capacity and behaviour.

Achieve the benefits of supervision within an embodied organisation by seeking a safe and supportive space (ideally with a mentor) to reflect on your work, your personal triggers and challenges in a non-judgmental way. Reflective practice and supervision can increase effectiveness, self-regulation and wellbeing – while addressing vicarious trauma, projection and abuse of power.

Where it is not working, these things will be happening:
- Leadership is not visible.
- Leadership withholds praise.
- Success is not celebrated.
- There is no choice of activity.
- There is no critical thinking or freedom of speech.
- There are no reflective or feedback procedures.
- No supervision.

Where it is working, these things will be happening:
- Leadership is visible, praise and celebrate success publicly, verbally and with gifts of time.
- Critical thinking is encouraged.
- All voices and views are sought and listened to.
- Supervision procedures are in place.

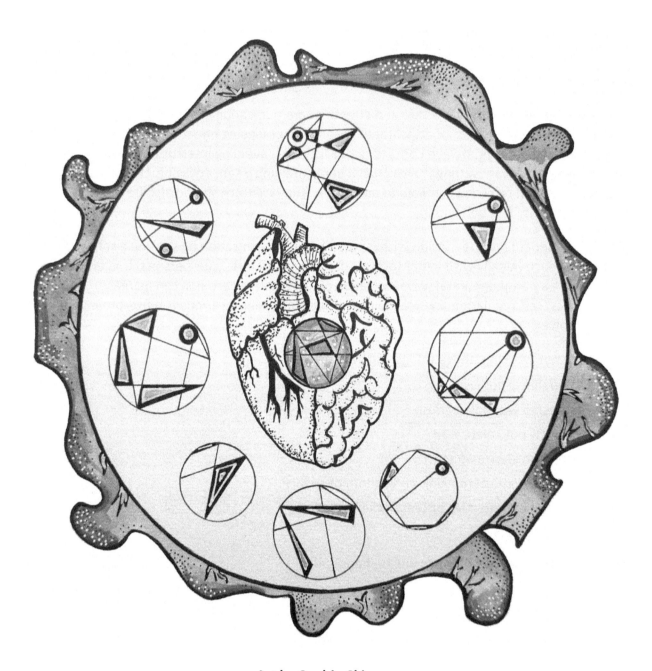

Art by Sophie Skinner

Body ABCs and Mind

BODY ABCs: Anchor. Breathe. Connect.

The content taught or delivered in an embodied organisation, educational space or trauma-informed curriculum will combine mind-based logical thinking and knowledge with wellness and nervous system embodiment education and strategies. There will be a logical structured scheme of learning which offers the basic foundational Body ABCs (anchor, breathe, connect) and nervous system strategies first.

Health and wellbeing education will play a crucial and central role in the learning process. Equally important will be the incorporation of knowledge and understanding about cyclical living, somatics, wellness, and the significance of regular rest.

In this context, emphasis will be placed on providing comprehensive education and resources related to maintaining physical and mental health. Additionally, the curriculum will include teachings on embracing the natural cycles of life, understanding the body-mind connection, prioritising wellness practices, and recognising the importance of regular rest for overall wellbeing.

Fostering a relationship between the mind and the body in learning and sharing spaces supports the development of self-leadership (more about this in the next section) and holistic learning – something the respondents of the informal questionnaire welcomed. When asked 'what is your view of the relationship between the mind and the body in education?', most had no direct experiences, but many commented on the value of this. Responses included 'moving the body is a release of tension, it clears the mind and heart', 'they should be treated as a whole', 'they are intimately connected', 'more attention should be paid to this', and 'you should nurture both equally in order to improve and utilise the education you are receiving'.

One participant offered a longer response to this question which offers an important reflection and enquiry around the power dynamics and battles played out on the body: 'the mind of children can't be educated unless their basic needs are met and unashamedly honoured.' Something as simple as needing the loo has become managed by being strict and rigid with permission giving. An argument from the system might be that some kids take advantage of going to the loo to get out of learning time, so it has to be controlled. This is an incredibly flawed argument, but even if that is the case, by not allowing free access to the bathroom the system is creating a self-perpetuating problem anyway. By restricting access to something so basic it becomes a novelty or privilege and then makes it more powerful – something to rebel against. If there's free access to something there is no power struggle, and it is no longer an issue. This is just one of many frustrating, flawed, and archaic practices that still exists in modern schools – and how power is wielded over our children to get them to conform'.

In a class or lesson, we can prepare the body and mind by taking a moment to pause before the learning starts. In this pause the students can be asked to implement the Body ABCs technique:

ANCHOR – feel their feet on the chair and bottom on the chair.

BREATHE – notice their breath.

CONNECT – place their hand on their stomach or heart to link mind and body.

This can happen after each activity and at any point in the session where you observe that the mind and body are out of sync. Learners can also write down their aims or intentions for the lesson. In addition, asking students to observe how the topic or activity made them feel physically supports embodied education. Enquiries such as did they have a reaction to the lesson topic and if so what type of reaction or feeling was generated? This helps to ground the mind with the sensations and messages that the body is sending through acknowledgement, bringing balance and union.

The importance of balancing the needs of the body and mind will be centred, as will the importance of syncing with the seasons and the body's needs – and learning and living from reciprocity with nature. Therefore, embodied, trauma-informed and safe facilitation offers an invitation of considering both/and – content which appeals to the body and mind and their preferred pathways of learning and being – linear content and cyclical/creative content – logic and intuitive, instinctive content.

As outlined in *The Foundational Basics* section, an embodied organisation is based on nervous system education, so it is imperative that the content below be taught and shared with all participants in the group. In planning or preparing sessions it is important to consciously build in time and space to allow these exercises where needed.

Supporting the Body to Support the Nervous System – Laying Foundations for Embodied Education

Titration is essential.

The concept of titration impresses upon us that less is more. Highly charged events, activities, ideas and content need to be titrated into the space – drip by drip. Delivering content, activities, and discussion in a 'slow and steady' stream (allowing for pause and integration) supports the nervous system.

Routine regulation of emotions and stress is essential.

Ensuring that those in the space stay in their body when the stress response is activated is helped by teaching everyone basic exercises to support themselves. Integrating these (along with aforementioned **ABC technique**) into lessons and meetings –so they become routine and reflexive – lays the foundations for embodied education.

Exercise 1: The SOS

This SOS exercise is designed to bring the body, mind and nervous system into a more contained and manageable state. It reduces anger, fear, panic, stress, anxiety, procrastination and avoidance.

The photo shows how to do the exercise – right hand goes under the left armpit and left hand around the top of the right arm. It seems so simple and yet its self-soothing and regulating effects are powerful and support the body to feel held, witnessed, and contained. We can also say kind words at the same time, such as 'may I be safe' or 'may I be peaceful'. This makes the exercise more impactful.[29]

---

[29] For further information, read *In An Unspoken Voice* by Peter A Levine.

Exercise 2: Building Capacity

Committing to regular facilitation of this embodied mindfulness technique will also expand the nervous system capacity of those in the space. Whenever there is a stress response in the body:

- Pause and feel it!
- Notice the sensations in your body.
- Listen to your breath.
- Feel feet on the ground.
- Bring your attention to your hands.
- Notice your pelvis, legs, and feet.
- Orient – look around your environment.

Exercise 3: The Maintenance – ongoing regular practice

Self-holding exercises, when done daily, empty the body's stress pot.

Placing the palm of the hand on different areas of the body, particularly the stomach, heart, forehead, back of the head, and nape, serves to provide a sense of containment, regulation, and active listening to the body.

This simple practice allows for a physical connection with these specific areas, creating a comforting and grounding effect. By gently placing the palm of the hand on these regions, individuals can enhance their awareness of bodily sensations, promote self-soothing, and foster a sense of being attuned to their own needs.

These exercises can be done during rest breaks or pauses in meetings, lessons, or sessions.

Exercise 4: Types of Breathing for Calm and Regulation

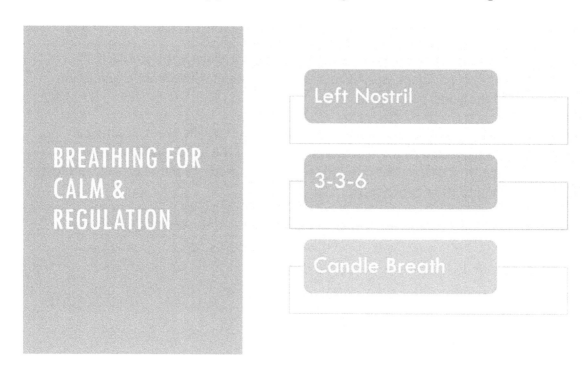

BREATHING FOR CALM & REGULATION

Left Nostril

3-3-6

Candle Breath

Left Nostril Breathing: Creates calmness, emotional balance and lowers blood pressure.

- Sit comfortably.
- **Close your right nostril** with your right thumb with your other fingers stretched straight up as antennas.
- Close your eyes if it feels good to do so.
- Begin to **breathe long and deep** only through your left nostril. Continue for **three minutes**.

3-3-6 Breath: Creates a deep experience of relaxation, calms anxieties, fear, and worry.

- **Inhale:** Breathe the air very slowly into the lungs for 3 seconds.
- **Hold:** Sustain the breath as you relax the chest and shoulders for 6 seconds.
- **Exhale:** Release the breath very slowly for 6 seconds.

Practice at the start of lessons, sessions, or meetings.

Candle Breath: Creates relaxation, lowers heart rate and the stress response.

- Inhale deeply.
- Exhale through the mouth – imagine that you are blowing out candles in front of you.

Exercise 5: Teach those in the space to know their 'go-to' resources.

Resources are things, or techniques, we use to bring more pleasure and regulation to the nervous system. They are actions which support self-soothing. What works for our nervous system is individual to us. Here are some examples:

- Titration – less is more. Go 'slow and steady'
- Boundaries – follow the body's lead when setting them
- Grounding techniques
- Breathing techniques (see examples in Exercise 4)
- Blankets
- Essential oils
- Orient yourself – look around and notice your current environment – floor to ceiling, ground to sky – panoramic, colours, objects, smells, everything
- Track body sensations and listen to what they are saying, how they are responding
- Self-touch – connect to skin and different parts of the body (examples are provided in Exercise 3)

Supporting the Mind to Support the Nervous System – Laying the Foundations for Embodied Education

Exercise 1: Mindfulness

Being in the 'now' in an embodied way soothes and builds capacity in the nervous system. It is a simple practice of noticing with curiosity and being aware of thoughts, feelings, and body sensations, while remaining connected to the world around us.

Exercise 2: Self-Coaching Technique

This response to stress involves cognitively assessing our response to a threat, trigger, or stressor.

To effectively reduce stress, we can explore four different responses. Two of these responses are external, namely "avoid" and "alter." These involve assessing if we can change the situation or circumstances that are causing stress.

The other two responses are internal, referred to as "adapt" and "accept." These involve evaluating whether we can modify our own reactions and responses to the stressful situation.

By considering these four responses—avoid, alter, adapt, and accept—we can better understand how to navigate and manage stress. It allows us to assess both external factors and our internal capacity to respond in a way that promotes resilience and wellbeing.

Think about the stressor and consider if you can…

Avoid it:

- Take control of your surroundings
- Avoid people who bother you
- Learn to say no
- Reduce the length of your 'to do' list

Alter it:

- Respectfully ask others to change their behaviour
- Communicate your feelings openly
- Manage your time better
- State limits in advance

Adapt to it:

- Adjust your standards
- Practice thought stopping
- Reframe the issue, see the learnings for example
- Adopt a mantra
- Assess the benefits of it
- Look at the big picture. Will it still matter in five years' time?

Accept it... whilst asking how can I support myself to move through this?

- Talk with someone
- Forgive – which means release yourself from the situation/person. Give it or them no more of your energy
- Practice kind self–talk
- Learn from your mistakes

Exercise 3: Teach and discuss the wellness model outlined earlier in the manual.

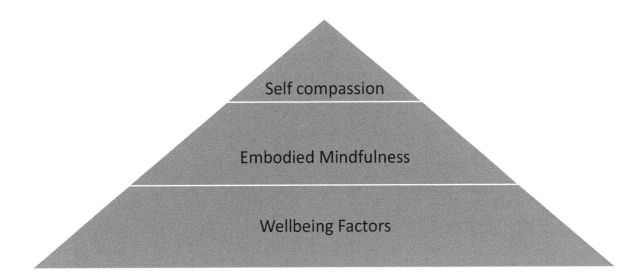

The base – the foundations of this wellness model – are factors which support wellbeing. These include:

- Nutrition which suits you
- Hydration
- Movement
- Functional breathing
- Restorative sleep
- Daylight
- Being in nature
- Health giving physical environment
- Time out for self to recharge
- Sense of identity
- Sense of meaning
- Emotional resilience
- Ability to ask for help
- Creativity
- Supportive, non-abusive relationships
- Social connection

Once these factors are in place and working well, we can really begin to feel the benefit of a regular **embodied mindfulness** practice, as outlined earlier. Remember that those in the space know themselves and their own body, so they may want to experiment or have other ideas.

The top of this wellness model is **self-compassion**. As explained earlier, this is the action of extending compassion to oneself in instances of perceived inadequacy, failure, or general suffering. It is being our own best friend and loving parent. Kristin Neff has defined self-compassion as being composed of three main components – self-kindness (not self-judgment), common humanity (not isolation) and mindfulness (not over-identification). There is a link to Kristen Neff's website in the *Further Exploration* section of this manual but if you would like to experiment now with a self-compassion practise try this:

Exercise 4: Self-compassion practise

Place hands on your heart and say these words:

May I be...

- Safe
- Peaceful
- Kind to myself
- Accepting of myself

Future Visioning: Try This – Embedding the Nervous System and Body Basics

1. *How does your community, or you as a teacher or facilitator safeguard against dissociation and ensure that everyone's stress response is as low as it can be at the start of meetings or sessions?*

2. *How does the content delivery and curriculum address education about the body and nervous system?*

3. Consider making it policy and procedure to do a breathing exercise or the ABC exercise at the start of meetings and session. Trialling this for six weeks to see the outcome may support those who are resistant to take part.

Self-Leadership

Organisations that prioritise embodiment, create safe and trauma-informed spaces and foster self-leadership and independent thinking. They do not create learned helplessness, dependency on the facilitator as the 'font of all knowledge' or encourage addictive behaviour in relation to the content or modalities taught or facilitated. Instead, the content supports resilience, inner discernment and the judgment of the participant or learner.

There is a conditioned expectation and assumption that teachers or those facilitating know everything – they are the 'expert' and are always 'right'. It is this belief that leads to student learned helplessness, where students cease to think for themselves and passively wait to be 'spoon-fed' information and knowledge. The education system does not support students to challenge this assumption or point out that the teacher has made an error. Accordingly, students will often 'blindly follow' the teacher– even if they disagree with them or know the content being delivered is factually not correct – as this keeps them 'safe', accepted and 'achieving'. The current system of education shuts down free thinking and encourages compliance, following whatever the teacher, the exam board and ultimately the government requests, requires or states.

To have unrestricted or free thinking, the leader or teacher must have the agenda to educate but not control, dictate or brainwash according to their own or 'mainstream' opinion. This entails that the facilitator or leader promotes the examination of diverse perspectives, considering multiple sources of evidence, and encouraging the use of critical thinking skills. These aspects will be further explored in subsequent discussions.

The teacher has to be adaptable – planning and tailoring content and learning activities to meet the group's needs and building in time for sharing, questioning and reflection. One positive change is that Ofsted has moved away from a single preferred teaching style, acknowledging that teaching and learning takes place in a variety of forms and ways.

Teaching that fosters independent thinking and self-leadership promotes doubt, reflection, adaptability, innovative interpretation, an internal locus of control, and internal validation. It also embraces the ability to accept constructive criticism from individuals within the learning environment. The primary goal is not to be "right," but rather to encourage exploration, curiosity, and understanding.

Facilitating an environment which encourages self-leadership is a trauma-informed approach, pioneered therapeutically by Richard C. Schwartz, the founder of Internal Family Systems (IFS) [30]. More about IFS can be accessed via the suggested source in the *Further Exploration* section at the end of this manual. The IFS model is a trauma therapy model which suggests that every mind has a variety of parts – which all have valuable skills – however it is the core Self which needs to lead, negotiate and bring integration and harmony to the individual.

---

[30] https://ifs-institute.com/

IFS is a therapeutic approach, one that embodied education and trauma-informed facilitation can learn from. It can also support the wholeness of a person – and consequently their wellbeing and personal power – by delivering content in a way which strengthens Core Self Leadership. This is done by promoting what IFS calls **the eights Cs of self-leadership:**

1. Calmness
2. Confidence
3. Creativity
4. Courage
5. Compassion
6. Curiosity
7. Connectedness
8. Clarity

Future Visioning: Try This – Self-Leadership

The following technique can be used in community meetings, lessons or any facilitated space.

Ensure each participant has a piece of paper and a pencil.

Ask participants to tune into the part of themselves that is calm, confident, creative, courageous, compassionate, curious, connected – and has clarity.

Ask them to explore it in the following ways:

- *What colour is it?*
- *Where is it in the body?*
- *Does it have a shape?*
- *Does it have a name?*
- *How old is it?*
- *If it were an animal, what would it be?*
- *What does it like to eat?*
- *What does it like to wear?*

Then extend the technique to the lesson, meeting or gathering. Ask what this part of self thinks about the idea, concept or point being discussed.

Creativity

As human beings we are not meant to perpetually copy – we are meant to create, to innovate, to birth something new, to evolve. Creativity facilitates problem solving, open mindedness and collaboration. Creativity spontaneously arises from being in the parasympathetic portion of the nervous system and so both flourishes and originates from, whilst also perpetuating, wellness.

Creativity, perhaps paradoxically, needs structure and tutelage, openness and freedom.

Research now tells us that we require a level of skill or mastery to cultivate creativity. This mastery might require some 10,000 hours of experience or *copying*. For example, an artist might spend hours perfecting their brush technique, then use the technique in their paintings. Musicians learn scales and chord progressions and this support them when they are writing music or `improvising a solo.

In addition, creativity is an organic process and part of innate body intelligence. It is also the innovation and originality which arises through the imaginative process. In creating, we conceive, gestate and birth something new and of value, which offers possibilities and solutions. Creating nourishes the body and facilitates joy, satisfaction, excitement, meaning and purpose – all essential to wellness.

Creativity is driven by the impulse to move, and its essence lies in movement propelling itself. The natural activation of the nervous subsystem, transitioning from the parasympathetic state to sympathetic action, represents the creative process. There is no force, control or expectation – it is the participant's body leading itself toward its desire and fire. Creativity flows when the individual is moved to move themselves, so it propagates autonomy and sovereignty. It is the urge of life-giving life to life!

Facilitating creativity involves allowing pauses for reflection on content, destruction and rejection – making space – moving past the old into a new idea and process – so creative content is cyclical and not static, and without expected outcome.

There is no embodied organisation or safe, trauma-informed learning and facilitation without creativity. Therefore, if the nervous system needs to be in a calm state to be creative, the question has to be asked as to whether educational environments cultivate the calm state for creativity to flourish. As discussed earlier, the majority of respondents to the informal questionnaire experienced stress in education environments.

The survey went on to ask the question, 'What was the impact of the education system and schooling on your creativity?' The responses were mixed as this participant explained, 'It helped and hindered.' Some respondents were positive, emphasising the tutelage and structure they received which supported creative development. Comments included, 'School gave me a firm foundation from which I could write, create, draw, tell stories', 'I loved art and had a great art education', 'I had a wonderful performing arts teacher who really allowed me to express myself creatively', 'An amazing art teacher who inspired me and championed my creativity', and 'Some teachers encourage it'.

The majority of other respondents weren't so positive. Comments included, 'Creativity wasn't encouraged, it was all about goal setting towards achieve and exam performance,' 'School destroyed much of the creative part of my childhood. I was so afraid of doing it wrong I stopped trying', 'It was suppressed', 'It stopped it', 'It's been nearly 10 years since sixth form and I am only just allowing my creativity to flow and have its place again', 'Limited and thwarted, particularly as a male', 'Nearly destroyed me', 'That creativity wasn't going to get you a 'good job', 'I ended up being someone who said I'm not creative' and 'put me off creative subjects I was forced to do them in a certain way to please teachers'.

Choice in content – options – is a vital part of embodied education and trauma-informed facilitation. In order to achieve wellbeing, it is essential for each individual to pursue their authentic desires. These visceral yearnings serve as their creative fuel and contribute to their overall wellness. Within the intensity of their special interest and desires, is their lifeforce, alignment, joy and unique contributions to the world. However, this approach is the direct opposite of the linear education system where learning is expected to take place during the one-hour lesson. Progress is tracked and has to be made by a particular time or point in the lesson. This is expected to be the same for all the students in the class – that they all reach the same point at the same time.

Time out in nature – freedom and play – support individuals to access their creativity and wellbeing too. Many participants emphasised the importance of nature-based time for effective learning, wellbeing and creativity.

Future Visioning: Try This – Integrating Creativity

Creating pauses in content delivery – stretches of free time (without electronics) in nature – can allow the creative flow to increase. Offering a stimulus can help, especially if these restful and explorative states are rare for individuals or groups.

In community gatherings or lessons, offer a couple of sessions outside. A stimulus to activate creative flow might be to spend five minutes looking around you. Notice which natural objects catch your eye.

Ask yourself why this is? What message might they have for you? What do they represent?

Language

This section will discuss the language of the content being taught or facilitated and the importance of it. Words shape culture, beliefs, thought forms and people. Words are powerful – and since language, at the moment, is the preferred ethos of communication – a trauma-informed approach to language is essential.

The philosopher Ludwig Wittgenstein said of language, "the limits of my language mean the limits of my world."[31] Language can empower. There is a saying – if you can't see yourself, you can't be yourself. If people of our gender, ethnicity or other demographic do not hold positions of power and leadership or feature within the content and curriculum delivered, then we have no role models, no roadmap and no visible pathway to be in our power or leadership.

The film director Federico Fellini said, "A different language is a different vision of life."[32] Our language and what we say creates our reality and the reality of those around us. It is useful to consider the way that we are using the language or words that we are expressing and communicating to students through them. For example, powerful language around the leadership and worth of women as well as men is essential. Being mindful of how we speak about men and women is an aspect of trauma-informed and safe facilitation. Being conscious that the language we use can literally spell the reality of people's lives and perpetuate disempowering narratives means that as space holders, teachers and leaders we need to be accountable and responsible for this.

The survey asked the question, 'Was your experience of learning about the Feminine and Goddess withing your schooling? Most answered 'none' or 'non-existent.' There was some mention of goddesses in art history or ancient history or classics – but that they were 'purely mythological beings. There was one significant longer share, which explained, 'Femininity was girly, despised, something the popular/pretty girls did – and consequently to be strongly avoided. The Greek (and to a much lesser degree, Norse) goddesses were the only 'goddess' I learned about, and they were just the social definition of Woman writ large: either hysterical and over-emotional, confusingly fixated on virginity or sluts who deserved their unpleasant ends, it was the gods that got to do fun, powerful, strong things – no goddesses.'

This is especially so in spiritual and wellness forums. Checking in with the current language and belief system of people in the space is vital. Assuming God or Goddess is the word everyone uses can be traumatising for those who have experienced religious abuse or brain washing. Stereotyping language around gender identity, behaviour and roles is also not trauma-informed facilitation. Checking preferred name and pronouns is. Adaptation to the language system of those in the space is vital.

---

[31] https://www.oxfordreference.com/display/10.1093/acref/9780191826719.001.0001/q-oro-ed4-00011662;jsessionid=EFBC2301D4932E1762D4792F6D14AF10
[32] shorturl.at/tFTUV

Trauma-informed language is not manipulative or coercive or confrontational. It has firm boundaries around how language is used by all members of the group and reminds us that energy follows intention and intentions spoken hold power. Reciprocity is cultivated alongside the knowing that compassionate language is clear and has boundaries – specific, direct, positive, and uses 'I' statements to take ownership of what is being expressed and conscious.

Using inclusive language and checking preferred pronouns is an important aspect of trauma-informed facilitation. It ensures that everyone in the group feels seen, respected, and acknowledged. It involves avoiding assumptions and makes a conscious effort to use appropriate pronouns when referring to individuals, fostering an inclusive and supportive environment for all.

Trauma sensitive language is nonaggressive and does not objectify. There is due care applied when topics such as abuse, violence , self-harm or suicide are spoken about and excessive details are not shared, which could trigger flashbacks. This needs careful management in wellness and spiritual sharing spaces or circles. Trauma-informed language is non commanding and offers invitations instead. Words and phrases are selected carefully and pathologising is avoided. Using language such as 'overwhelm', 'dysregulation', 'seeking nurturance and reassurance', 'soothing', 'discomfort', 'distress', 'seeking boundaries and predictability', 'disconnect' and 'seeking acceptance' are all better than using the words 'attention seeking', 'ungrateful', 'sabotages', 'controlling', 'clingy', 'anxious' or 'overreacting'.

Future Visioning: Try This – Masculine and Feminine

- Exploring ideas around concepts of masculine and feminine is an important aspect of trauma-informed and safe facilitation.
- In community meetings or the spaces, you facilitate exploration and discussion of these words – without judgement. Understanding viewpoints, triggers and disempowerment has created safe space.

Undo the Patriarchy

Patriarchy has been defined as "A society in which the oldest male is the leader of the family, or a society controlled by men in which they use their power to their own advantage" [33]

A patriarchal organisation or space is neither trauma-informed nor safe. Patriarchal dynamics and ethos, thoughts and beliefs are so embedded into our psyche, behaviour, actions and language that, at times, it is hard to recognise. As long as patriarchy is part of an institution, community, learning or sharing space there is *power over, oppression and abuse.*

It is also useful to consider what the impact might be with replacing patriarchy with matriarchy. All systems and structures have apparent advantages and disadvantages but also have the potential to alienate different groups of people. The key to adopting a suitable structure for your space is to reduce or remove bias. The findings demonstrated that sexism is ingrained in the education system. One participant commented, 'Thank you for giving me the opportunity to complete this. At 50 and a very different person to my teenage self I only now realise how biased the education system was and how fortunate I was to achieve what I did with the odds stacked against me as a girl. I hadn't realised just how male biased the education system was but also how the projected inferiority of girls was so ingrained'.

The survey asked two questions:

1. What were you taught about woman?
2. What were you taught about man?

Answers to Question 1 included the following comments: 'I don't remember anything positive', 'Mary!', 'conform to social norms', 'in an all-boys school nothing was taught', 'female characters in classics, e.g., Emma and female biblical characters who benefitted from Jesus' miracles - we were not taught about actual people', 'body parts', 'homemakers', 'I attended an all-girls school and we were told girls could do anything', 'a woman is either a worthless whore or a virtuous virgin', 'that we are lesser, temptress, we don't feature in history, religion, art, in fact most things', 'female form in art' and 'carer'.

Answers to Question 2 included these comments: 'I suppose that they were generally the first to do things, the ones who invented things, the top dog', 'they had the advantage', 'most historical figures were male', 'most significant figure were man in all subjects', 'that you would want to find a good one and marry them!' 'try to be one, not a wimp', 'biology,' 'they were gods', 'nothing except to keep away from them', 'men are superior to women physically and mentally, but women are more moral and nurturing', 'the whole curriculum centred on the achievements and legacy of men', 'he's dominant', 'power' and 'run the world'.

---

[33] https://dictionary.cambridge.org/dictionary/english/patriarchy

Learning and sharing spaces need to start to address this continued misogyny and patriarchal bias. How to do this is an ongoing enquiry but a starting point has to be gender positive messages for all, role models, and gender inclusivity in curriculum content.

The following information is to provide a starting point for reflection and to assess the extent to which the patriarchy is alive and active in the organisation you are part of, or the space you hold, and the content being delivered. Women perpetuate the patriarchy when they centre male experience and, particularly white men's needs and also when they contribute to male privilege and power or use their own power for their own advantage, extracting from others in doing so.

Is the content you deliver your creation and is your delivery authentic? Are you in integrity in relation to it? Part of patriarchy is extractivism – using someone or something for our own gain an advantage so if any aspect of the content you deliver is copied – extracted from someone else's creation – then patriarchy is active within the space. There is a difference between being inspired and deliberately copying or extracting information, practices and so on from others or another culture with reciprocal exchange.

Have you checked the integrity of your sources? Have you critiqued and explored other viewpoints? Are you able to offer the content as an invitation, rather than an absolute? Have you checked in around the cultural appropriateness of the content and around any bias? Is there history and herstory?

Are you checking that how you facilitate and the content itself is nervous system friendly and embodied? – i.e., that there is no spiritual bypassing or harm?

Are you safeguarding against cult dynamics and power over dynamics – subliminal messages in the content? Have you assessed the undercurrent and programmed messages in the content?

Have you assessed the extent to which the content perpetuates oppressive systems, such as the patriarchy and its associated theories, practices, and -isms, listed below? To what extent are any of the following listed item's part of the content you deliver, the space you hold or the community or institution you are part of or lead?

- Hyper individualism – acting out in a self-serving way, without any regard for others or wider society.
- White fragility – the defensive reaction of a white individual and the discomfort they experience when discussing racism, or racial inequality.
- White supremacy – belief in the superiority and therefore entitled dominance and control of white individuals in society.
- Misogyny – contempt, ingrained prejudice and dislike against women.
- Privilege – advantage of a person.
- Prejudice – pre-judgement, preconceive opinion note based on actual experience.

- Discrimination – acting on prejudice – unjust treatment due to race, age, gender disability, ethnicity.

- Sexism – prejudice, discrimination and stereotyping due to gender.

- Racism – prejudice, discrimination, stereotyping and marginalisation of an ethnic group.

- Colonialism – One national controlling the people and land of another for economic gain.

- Capitalism – an economic system where private individuals or organisations own the means of production for their own individual profit.

- Consumerism – society's preoccupation with acquiring and purchasing goods for personal gratification and economic boost.

- Elitism – Dominance, rule and leadership by an elite (small group of powerful people with disproportionate power, privilege, wealth, skill, opportunities, contact, connections).

- Extractivism – extracting earth's (or another person's) resources (or ideas and content) to sell.

- Ableism – discrimination which favours able-bodied people.

Future Visioning: Try This – No One Person's Fault and Everyone's Responsibility

- The origins of patriarchy are complex and not for this manual[34]. What is certain is that patriarchy perpetuates trauma and unsafety and so assessing our parts in this and acting to create change is essential if we are to offer safe space.

- Examining and reflecting on this can be difficult and the above process is not meant to shame or blame. Whilst it is not our fault that we are in this paradigm in the world if we want to be fully trauma-informed and create impactful change it is all our collective responsibility to assess and make changes to content and facilitation practices.

- Based on this section of the manual, what content do you feel you need to amend in your facilitation or community?

---

[34] For more information, read *The Creation of Patriarchy* by Gerda Lerner.

Navigating the Change – What it Looks Like in Practice

Use language to support the creation of a safe space by being mindful and respectful in communication. This can include avoiding harmful language or behaviour, actively listening, and avoiding assumptions. Language can also help establish clear boundaries, expectations and guidelines for behaviour. Using inclusive language, avoiding stereotypes and promoting equality can also contribute to creating a safe environment for all. In a safe space, open and non-judgmental communication is encouraged, allowing individuals to express themselves freely and be heard.

To actively work to avoid perpetuating patriarchy in organisations, communities, or learning and sharing spaces, it is important to adopt gender-positive messages and be inclusive in curriculum content. When delivering content, it should be authentic, critically assessed for sources, bias, cultural appropriateness, and harm to the nervous system. Delivery should be an invitation, not content set in stone. Before you begin always check for oppressive systems or norms such as hyper individualism, white fragility, white supremacy, misogyny, homophobia, and ableism. The content should also be assessed for undercurrent and programmed messages and safeguarded against cult dynamics and power over dynamics. The goal is to reduce or remove bias and create a safe and trauma-informed space for all.

Where it is not working, these things will be happening:

- No somatic practices happening
- Capacity not honoured – people push through
- Talking over emotional expression
- Creativity discouraged
- Patriarchy denied.

Where it is working, these things will be happening:

- Somatic practices integrated into day-to-day work
- Day to day capacity and regulatory capacity honoured
- Breathing techniques modelled and encourages
- Preferred resources available
- Coaching approaches to support and leadership
- Wellness embedded in culture
- Creativity encouraged and celebrated
- Active deconstruction of patriarchal practices and culture

Art by Sophie Skinner

Creative Curiosity

Learning is not linear. Instead, it is a creative process – messy, looping and doubling back are usual. Facilitating via methods which encourage curiosity, discovery and self-directed exploration encourage creative learning and empower.

Being a creative facilitator and space holder, demonstrating and modelling curiosity and creative leadership, alongside being flexible and adapting to the preferences of those in the space, all fosters a culture of creative curiosity.

The informal survey showed that participants felt an effective facilitator or teacher keeps 'students engaged and excited about learning,' 'is creative and has presence' and 'makes learning a joy.' Respondents also offered these preferences for ways to learn: 'independent, free-wheeling, non-sequential', 'self-directed', variety of activities, independent and collaborative', 'physically get involved', 'sitting on the floor, food and drinks when needed', 'visual aids, books and videos', 'in comfy clothes', 'nature-based', 'exploratory environments', 'listening to people talk about something they are passionate about', 'going down rabbit holes of a larger subject' 'practically' and 'a mix of self-study and mentoring'.

Creative curiosity is participant and student-led facilitation and learning. It is self-directive. The role of the teacher and space holder is to scaffold and offer boundaries for the creative process to take place. Without stimulus or boundaries for the exploration, creative energy can be difficult to channel.

Curiosity is at the centre of creative facilitation and leadership of embodied learning organisations. Rewarding curiosity, even when critiquing and encouraging exploration – including exploration of thoughts, feelings, and inner knowing – is part of this type of pedagogy. The key is to keep the focus on questions – not answers – and making connections so project-based learning and enquiries are useful. Mistakes will be praised – as is 'failure' which will be reframed as first attempt at learning. Thinking for self and resilience are developed through this pedagogy and actively encouraging the freedom to disagree or debate all established theories stimulates curiosity. Independent and original thinking are central to it.

Facilitating creative curiosity is non-authoritarian, non-dictatorial and non-patriarchal – there is room for all ideas and view. Differences are accepted and so there is an atmosphere of inclusion and collaboration. Changing perspectives and views – adaptation and amendment – are celebrated.

A variety of methods to access creative curiosity can be deployed – doing, being, listening, imagining, drawing, writing, doodling, makings, building, moving – so that mind, body and energy work together as was explained earlier. This is the amalgamation of metacognition, intuition and instinct. Critical thinking is deployed in curiosity through a compare and contrast method of alternative perspectives and views – and included in the analysis is the inner knowing and internal guidance of all participants. There is no fear-based rhetoric or learning, and no checking out of the body.

Future Visioning: Try This – Creative Curiosity

1. Create space in facilitation for the discovery of new knowledge and experience – for novelty. *How can novelty be part of your community or learning environment?*

2. Discuss this with the group and encourage:

   - People to sit in different seats or spaces
   - Brainstorming or mind map solutions
   - The creation of mood or vision boards for discussion topics

Always ask the participant what their mind thinks, what their body feels, and what emotions want you to do about a question or idea.

Critical Thinking

Critical thinking is a vital skill to teach, facilitate and encourage in embodied organisations. It supports individuals to keep themselves safe, to discern and to develop their own value and belief system – thereby facilitating their autonomy over their lives. Critical thinking safeguards against gaslighting, abuse, indoctrination and brainwashing. Any arena which forbids or even discourages critical thinking is not trauma-informed or safe.

Critical thinking revolves around asking questions – not to be awkward, combative, attacking or affronting – rather instead to be open, explorative and curious. As one respondent in the informal questionnaire suggested, 'design a curriculum which focuses on educating people about human beings, our emotions, as well as developing critical young people, not obedient, subservient subjects to be controlled in later life.'

Critical thinking promotes problem solving and creativity – allowing for analysis and adjustment and growth. It is a transferable skill – growing individuals in all areas of their life not just facilitated space – as the skill can be applied in a variety of life scenarios, circumstances and situations.

Facilitating critical thinking involves using symbol and analogy, encouraging discussion and sharing of ideas, encouraging reflection and research, applying to real-life settings and situations, encouraging 360 degrees thinking and perspective, encouraging change, viewing purpose, gathering information, thinking about assumptions, implications and inferences and critiquing bias, hidden meaning.

Scepticism is important but so is humility and the willingness to listen and be curious before formulating view or judgment. Sometimes it is really useful in discussions or projects to encourage students to research and present a view or perspective which is different than their own. A multi-faceted sharing can birth innovation and collaboration – as well as tolerance and acceptance of difference – which in turn creates safety.

The facilitator is essential to the success of critical thinking. As one comment from the findings explained, an effective teacher 'can teach their subject in a way that brings the student with them, whatever their level of understanding, is enthusiastic and actively involves students in their own learning. They empower you to answer a question and if you got it totally wrong would ask supplementary questions to bring you to the right answer, instilling confidence in learning. The worst teachers dismissed your answer with a level of contempt when you got it wrong, so you didn't want to answer next time.'

Future Visioning: Try This – The importance of open-ended questions

Critical thinking revolves around exploration and asking open-ended questions. In community meeting or when leading a sharing or learning space, pay attention to the questions you ask.

Can you ensure questions are open-ended? What happens when you do?

Starting questions with how or one of the three W's will support you to ask an open-ended question:

> *What... ?*
>
> *Where... ?*
>
> *Why... ?*

Storytelling

Why is storytelling an important pedagogical approach in embodied learning organisations and sharing spaces? Mainly because storytelling creates connection and inspires – it creates a sense of sharing, commonality and unity. In addition, storytelling opens the mind and body up to thoughts, words, images and somatic sensations – journeys us into a wider understanding of the world and experiences of those in other cultures or demographics. Storytelling helps us access our deeper knowing (intuition and instinct) and creates emotional connection and empathy and compassion. It also helps us feel less alone in our experiences and can offer us hope and pathways out of difficulty, as we read about others who have overcome the adversity we have faced. So, storytelling can be healing.

The responses collected as part of the research process highlighted the longing for this to be integrated into learning. Participants suggestions included 'less mandatory literature', 'community instead of individualism', 'create education villages' and 'emotional intelligence education'.

However, stories need to be told in a trauma-sensitive way. Sharing graphic details or horror, violence and abuse is not safe facilitation. Storytelling provides a pathway to accessing the unconscious mind and self, and for some, even the Soul. Therefore, it is crucial to approach it with caution and ensure a safe facilitation process.

Storytelling allows for exploration. of values and beliefs in an 'impersonal' way, boosts active listening and imagination, increases tolerance and cultural awareness, improves communication and social skills and can support memory and learning. Through stories we can imagine something new – a different way or path or alternative perspective. Stories also generate creative enthusiasm and encourage further exploration.

Stories are powerful in persuasion – they inform and can 'implant' programmes and beliefs into our minds. Trauma-informed facilitation will ensure that story telling is done with integrity, alongside the deployment of critical thinking and metacognition. Sharing a powerful narrative of recovery, healing, or a religious/spiritual myth can have a significant impact, evoking a sense of conviction and inspiring commitment to the belief system or wellness approach.

For safe and embodied education to take place, there needs to be story analysis and discussion of the belief and value systems, solutions and messages it entails. Making the implicit explicit. Storytelling can also trigger a somatic response – as an unconscious trauma could be triggered as the 'body' recognises the plight of another – so somatic exercises post storytelling and checking in with the body response to the story is especially useful for safe facilitation.

Creative writing and encouraging participants to share their personal stories hold tremendous power. By crafting and narrating creative stories, we have the ability to reshape the narratives of our own lives through the transformative force of imagination.

Future Visioning: Try This – What is the story of the body?

1. Encouraging the body to tell its story is a trauma-informed and embodied education practice.

At the start of meetings, sessions or lessons, invite participants to share the narrative of their body. Its colour, animal nature, preferences and where it's at. You'll get a quick sense of people's feelings, thoughts, capacity and needs that way.

Prompts:

If your body were to send a text message right now, what would it say?

If your body were a landscape, when would it be? Describe it.

Which song is playing in your body? Why has it chosen that song?

What is the weather system of your body today? Describe it.

If I was looking for your body on a restaurant menu, what would I read?

Metacognition

To facilitate the pedagogical approach of metacognition the facilitator encourages participants to develop awareness of their thinking and learning – what they think and how they learn.

Metacognition is often referred to as the process of thinking about one's own thinking and learning or thinking about how you think and learn. This means more than just simply accepting a fact or piece of knowledge. It involves you actively being aware of how the new information makes you feel: How does it fit in with what you already know? Does it challenge your current views and constructs? Why do I need to know this information? Where will I use it?

So why spend time thinking about your thinking? Metacognitive practices support the student to assess their own progression and since they are aware of this, they can take control of their learning. In some ways it is similar to being present.

Strategies useful for developing this include allowing those in the space to follow their own learning style – so giving time for movement, drawing, discussion, making and so on. Breaking down tasks and supporting planning, resourcing, researching. Reflecting on prior knowledge and understanding, errors or mistakes but also successes, with the intention of future adaptation. Scheduling and breaking down the process of the task or project and encouraging continual reflection and amendment. Asking questions is encouraged throughout projects or exploration.

Assessment, reflection, evaluation and adaptation are the key skills of metacognition.

Modelling guided and independent methodologies are key strategies for the facilitator to initiate. Seeking feedback from others and ensuring measurable and achievable mini goals to support periodic assessment is also an aspect of the pedagogy and is motivational.

Encourage learners to keep a learning journal as it is an effective method for them to monitor and develop their ability to reflect, to plan and to evaluate their learning and what the next steps they should take are. It supports them to think about how they think, and can encourage curiosity, concepts, make connections and form questions.

It is very useful for those in the space to understand how the brain actually works and the importance of nervous system regulation and embodiment to the clarity and outcome of thinking. Understanding neuroplasticity and that the brain is wired to grow helps the development of resilience and hope.

Thinking about thinking can be stimulated by existential or 'moral dilemma' questions – discussing the challenge of being human. Challenging bias creates flexibility.

The outcome of the findings of the responses collected for the manual demonstrates that the skills of metacognition are not predominant on the current schooling and organisational landscape. When asked 'if you could change three things about the education system what would they be and why?' respondents suggestions included, 'critical thinking and philosophy from reception all the way to leaving,' 'learning to learn,' 'allow for neurodivergent individuals and thinking' and 'teach mastery, *instead* of trying to rush through the scheme of learning'.

Future Visioning: Try This – Encouraging Reflection

Whether it occurs in a staff community meeting, a sharing session, or a teaching environment, providing opportunities for reflection throughout the year or course fosters metacognition. This can be facilitated through various means, such as journaling.

Prompt questions to ask at the beginning, middle and end of the meeting or course could be:

- *What do you now find easeful and why?*

- *What do you find challenging and why?*

- *How do you like to learn and why?*

- *What do you now know about yourself because of your learning/this discussion?*

- *What adaptations have you made and what was the outcome?*

- *If you were to do the task or have the discussion again, what might you do or say differently and why?*

Intuition

Making space in community meetings, sessions or sharing spaces for intuitive learning and activities is an aspect of trauma-informed and safe facilitation and embodied organisations. Giving time and space for people to tune into their innate knowing – their 'sixth sense' and then to share what these reveals in relation to the topic, activity or ideas being discussed is integral to embodied education.

Creating opportunities for participants to share their lightning fast 'hunches' – and comparing the response to gut instinct, evidence-based findings, other ideas or research – are holistic and integrative ways to lead, teach and space hold.

Currently what we heard was this is not happening in how we learn to learn. Words used by participants to describe their experience of school were 'monotonous,' 'restrictive', 'jungle', 'constrictive', 'diminishing' and 'stealing my headspace'. Only 3.8% selected the word 'intuitive' to describe their schooling.

When planning a session, it is important to build in reflection time and time for the individual to be with their thoughts. Also, to allow breaks between sessions as a time to unwind and then reflect. Many institutions, in order to be time and cost effective have reduced this time, instead replacing it with an extra lesson. Some schools in the States have a recommended 20 minutes for lunch. This leaves no time for reflection or even down time. Nutrition experts advise that 20 minutes is not enough for children to properly eat and digest their food before heading back to class.

As the space holder or leader of the space, being able to tune into our own intuition is a vital skill for trauma-informed facilitators – reading the room and adapting the facilitation pedagogy, methods or plans to the needs of the group creates safety and maintains engagement. It may also help to pick up safeguarding issues.

Teaching the group to trust their intuition in social situations creates self-belief, trust and protection. They self-affirm and cultivate inner worth and wisdom – their inner guidance compass is activated.

Pedagogical approaches which support community members and participants to engage with the intuition also helps them engaged with heart intelligence and playfulness – essential, for wellbeing. Developing and normalising tuning into intuition is done by making space for rest, unstructured time, listening to self, embodiment and conscious breathing, self-regulation exercises and using the language of intuition. Asking questions such as what do you feel? what is your heart telling you? what do you sense? what feels right for you? will help.

Future Visioning: Try This – Trauma-informed Guided Visualisation

As part of a project or inquiry into a topic, ask participants or community members to get clear in their heart-led intuitive response.

Do this by experimenting with trauma-informed and guided visualisation.

Trauma-informed practice requires that you ensure participants are 'in their body' before you begin – so going back and doing the Body ABCs technique and some breathing and grounding work from earlier in the manual will be needed.

The visualisation needs to also be done with eyes open:

1. Ground the participants.
2. Ask them to place one hand on their heart and the other on their leg.
3. Breathe together whilst asking the participants to orient – scan the room.
4. Ask the participants to imagine that the hand on their heart has a magic x-ray eye in the centre of it.
5. The eye can look into their heart for their intuitive answer to the question.
6. Ask them to sense what the answer or response is – saying that it might be words, colours, a shape, animal, or feeling, as intuition tends to be metaphorical and symbolic in communication.
7. Discuss their findings.

Instinct

70.4% of participants stated that they had considered their body as a vehicle for knowing and learning and yet there were no comments about this being part of or nurtured within their schooling or learning. As one participant stated, 'there was nothing about body wisdom' and another that it is 'totally absent in our education system but learning how to inhabit our bodies and navigate our emotions could and should play an integral part in educating young people'.

Facilitation and trauma-informed, safe learning and leadership creates space for and encourages the development of the personal instinct of the community – every individual in the space. Cultivation of a connection to instinct in participants develops self-leadership as their nervous system and body indicate the instinct to escape, self-assert, set boundaries (anger), repel and remove.

Encouraging participants to refer to their instincts and trust them, cultivates the ability to meet their own needs, self-soothe and regulate. Participants also learn instinct-based strengths – following the instinct to share. And play.

Instinct-based learning and facilitation requires the space holder to model how they follow and connect to their own instinct and to bring the language system on instincts into the space.

Future Visioning: Try This – Developing Instinct

- *Can emotions and body sensations be incorporated into facilitation methods?*

- *Can anger be safely explored?*

It is useful to try a method which trauma specialist Irene Lyon[35] calls the towel twist, to channel healthy aggression, feel the body sensation of it and see what those in the space learn about themselves from the exercise. Anger is a useful energy and instinct as it gifts us lifeforce, courage and strong boundaries of self-protection.

- Ensure all participants have a towel. Twist the towel whilst expressing sounds of anger – a gentle growl or snarl.
- Notice sensations on the back, shoulders, stomach, wrists and hands.
- Discuss the experience

---

[35] https://irenelyon.com/

Navigating the Change – What it Looks Like in Practice

Develop critical thinking as a skill to promote in your organisation. It helps individuals to protect themselves, understand their own values and beliefs, and maintain autonomy over their lives. By asking questions and encouraging exploration, critical thinking fosters creativity, problem-solving, and personal growth. Facilitating critical thinking involves using symbols, fostering discussion, conducting research, and promoting a wide range of perspectives. A key aspect of critical thinking is also scepticism combined with humility and openness to different views.

Strive to promote a holistic and integrative approach to learning and teaching, create space for intuitive learning and activities in meetings, sessions, or sharing spaces by allowing participants to tune into their innate knowing (sixth sense) and share their insights.

Breaks and reflection time should always be built into any session to promote unwinding and reflection. As the facilitator tune into your own intuition and adapt to the needs of the group which will create a safer and more engaging environment. Teach the group to trust their intuition in social situations to build self-belief, trust, and protection. Also try asking questions related to feelings, heart, and intuition, as this can help participants engage with their intuition and heart intelligence.

Where it is not working, these things will be happening:

- Creativity is discouraged.
- Intuition ignored.
- Emotions are pathologized

Where it is working, these things will be happening:

- Creativity is celebrated.
- There is a full spectrum of healthy emotional expression
- Storytelling
- Investigation of sixth sense
- Healthy aggression modelled and practised.

Conclusion

In this manual, we presented the model of Embodied Education (The Space, The Space Holder, The Content and The Pedagogy), alongside content to raise awareness and support curiosity of the issues surrounding it. We also suggested alternatives and solutions, strategies and practices for you to try out and consider.

Our intention in writing this manual was to provide a progressive paradigm which offers an alternative embodied organisational approach to learning, facilitation and space holding, rooted in safety, wellbeing, collaboration, creativity, and innovation – which we believe are the cornerstones to discovery and growth. This begins with an organisational ethos and value system, rich learning environments and resources, which all support diversity and create a space for all humans to flourish and thrive. These are settings where everyone in the space, facilitators, learners and participants alike, expand and develop a complete set of life skills, values and experiences that prepare them for a continuously shifting and unknown global future.

Thank you for reading.

We invite you to continue to create spaces where learning and facilitation takes place which are embodied (safe, trauma-informed and nervous system friendly) and in which:

- Individuality, divergence and innovation are valued, celebrated and encouraged.
- Exploration, discovery and creativity are the foundational values.
- Getting it wrong is getting it right, intuition is considered a *go point of reference* and above all else, gut instinct has the final say.

To accomplish this, we recommend that you continue to engage in repeated reading, experimentation, and integration of the contents into your personal and professional life. Embodiment is a skill that requires practice. Take time to reflect, adjust, and adapt as necessary.

Discuss this with those you teach, care for or hold space for. Connect with like-minded people. Do your own research and reading.

Above all – keep learning. Listen to your intuition and gut instinct. They will guide you.

Kay and Dan Aldred

Cover Art – Janus – by Andrew Swiatkowski

https://www.andrewswi.art/

IG @andrewswi

Janus is the god of endings and beginnings.

This image is a gateway, signifying a time of transitions, and the merging of duality.

We are opening the door to Embodied Education.

About the Artists

Andrew Swiatkowski is based out of Denver, Colorado. He is a mixed-media artist with a particular interest in acrylics and charcoals. Key themes of his art are spirituality and divine feminine energies. He studied in Aspen with Christine Anderson and has been making and selling work consistently for over 15 years.

A key element of his work draws upon the concept of having an introspective journey through your body and spirit to discover something good and new. It's a belief that one can pull these new concepts through the chaos and make it make sense. His work is also inspired by stories of the ancient past as well as images of ancient goddesses. The desire to make an old image and idea reborn and re-awakened through color and stylized movements.

You can find Andrew on IG @andrewswi and his website is https://www.andrewswi.art.

I am **Soph Skinner**, a 26-year-old creatrix.

Addicted to diving into the deeper, darker and elevated, angelic parts of my inner being through art and poetry. With all my creative outlets I am constantly transmuting and rebirthing myself to become all that I want to be. I'd love you to join me on this journey and share yours with me!

I specialise in graphic art, bringing your inner visions, dreams and desires to life in the physical realm.

As a poetry writer and lover, words are my main source of inspiration and always have been. This is why I work so closely with sigils. To me a sigil is a form of symbol that holds our intentions- we make an intention in words and by sealing it within a symbol it helps us take action to change our reality and manifest our desires in life. In my own ritual practices, I create an art work with each full and new moon.

You can find Sophie on Instagram at @she_who_creatrix and her website is https://shewhocreatrix.uk.

About the Authors

Kay Louise Aldred is a researcher, writer, and educator, who catalyses individual, institutional and collective evolution - through education, embodiment, and creativity - amalgamating metacognition, intuition, and instinct.

She has published three workbooks of her own with Girl God Books - *Mentorship of Goddess: Growing Sacred Womanhood, Making Love with the Divine: Sacred, Ecstatic, Erotic Experiences* and *Somatic Shamanism: Your Fleshy Knowing as the Tree of Life* - in addition to co-authoring *Embodied Education: Creating Safe Space for Learning Facilitating and Sharing* with her husband Dan Aldred. The couple reside in North Yorkshire, England.

www.kaylouisealdred.com
Instagram, Twitter and LinkedIn @kaylouisealdred

Dan Aldred is a Computer Science teacher, and a freelance resource writer and hacker. He has championed the use of the Raspberry Pi as a tool for learning and creativity, and is a Raspberry Pi Certified educator. Dan led the winning team of students for the first Astro Pi competition, whose code is now orbiting Earth aboard the ISS. Dan currently resides in the UK. Dan runs the website TeCoEd full of Raspberry Pi hacks and projects and also a You Tube channel.

If you enjoyed this book, please consider writing a brief review on Amazon and/or Goodreads! Thank you!

Further Exploration: Embodied Education

Connect with Us
Kay – www.kaylouisealdred.com @kaylouisealdred (Twitter, LinkedIn and Instagram)
Dan – https://www.tecoed.co.uk/ @Dan_Aldred (Twitter)

Understanding the Nervous System
Irene Lyon https://irenelyon.com/

Healing Trauma
Dr. Stephanie Mines created The TARA Approach, organized around promoting authentic nervous system health and resilience through the resolution of trauma, shock and any other obstacles to optimal development. http://www.tara-approach.org/

Shame
David Bedrick writes about unshaming. https://www.davidbedrick.com/

Polyvagal Theory
https://www.stephenporges.com/

Books
In An Unspoken Voice. How the Body Releases Trauma and Restores Goodness by Peter A Levine

Nurturing Resilience. Helping Clients Move Forward from Developmental Trauma. An Integrative Somatic Approach by Kathy L Kain and Stephen J Terrell

The Body Keeps the Score. Mind, Brain and Body in the Transformation of Trauma by Bessel Van Der Kolk

Waking the Tiger. Healing Trauma by Peter A Levine

More about Self Compassion
https://self-compassion.org/

More about Internal Family Systems
https://ifs-institute.com/

More about Schooling
A school that replaced Detention with Yoga https://bit.ly/3AqjXHr

When the Adults Change, Everything Changes: Seismic shifts in school behaviour by Paul Dix

Other books Mentioned in the Manual
A General Theory of Love, by Lewis, Amini and Lannon

Goddess Luminary Leadership Wheel A Post-Patriarchal Paradigm by Dr Lynne Sedgmore

Sacred Medicine: A Doctor's Quest to Unravel the Mysteries of Healing by Lissa Rankin

The Creation of Patriarchy by Gerda Lerner

More about Neurodivergence

https://ndconnection.co.uk/

Thanks to the Survey Respondents

Prior to writing this manual, we invited willing participants, via social media platforms, to share their formative experiences of schooling, learning and education from the perspective of student or teacher. We stated that their comments would be included as anonymised shares in this manual. We heard from a global audience of 56 respondents via an anonymous online survey over the period of one month – January to February 2022.

- 25% answered from the perspective of a teacher, 75% from a student perspective.
- Ages of participants ranged from 18 to 70+ years.
- 17.9% of participants identified as male and 82.1% identified as female.
- 82.1% of participants responded from the perspective of state school (the rest from the perspective of private, selective, free, faith and home school settings).

In addition, permission was given to Kay, from some of her private coaching clients and participants from workshops, courses and retreats, to anonymously share their wide variety of experiences of space holding and facilitation on courses, retreats, workshops, classes in a range of wellness, personal development and spiritual settings.

Thank you to all of those who so generously shared their raw, honest and inspirational stories and experiences via the anonymous online survey. Without your voices this book would not have been written.

Other Thanks

Thank you for **every student** we have had the privilege to teach or space-hold for.

Huge appreciation to the GGB publishing team; to **Trista** for her yes and tireless positivity and encouragement of the book and us personally, to **Pat** for her expert editing, and **Anders** for the fabulous front cover production. You are magic.

Huge thanks to **Andrew Swiatkowski** for generously allowing us to use your magnificent Janus painting for the cover art of the book.

Gratitude to **Sophie Skinner** for allowing us to include your stunning and magical art throughout the book and to **Grase McFarlane** for your poignant and powerful art and words.

And finally thank you, thank you, thank you for our quirky, divergent, creative and wise children, **James, Archie** and **Elizabeth**. May you live authentically, embody your truth and always be free.

Milton Keynes UK
Ingram Content Group UK Ltd.
UKHW011306240724
1019UKWH00032B/274